ANALYZING FINANCIAL INSTITUTIONS

Andrew G. Lacey

DISCLAIMER

The aim of this book is to provide a high standard of financial education to the reader, the calculations, ratios and models discussed aiming to give insight into the well-being of the particular firm being analyzed. However, when using this book, the reader acknowledges that the Author and Publisher cannot accept any responsibility for how the information is used to make financial and other decisions, this being the sole responsibility of the decision-maker. Also, while every effort has been made to keep the information accurate, the Author and Publisher cannot accept any liability for any unintentional errors. The reader should consider seeking independent advice before making (or refraining from making) any specific credit, investment, financial or other decision of material size. Companies and firms analyzed in the case studies within this book are fictional, though based on real firms with different names. Any similarity in names with real companies is purely co-incidental.

Contents

Chapter 1 10
INTRODUCTION BY THE AUTHOR 10
Chapter 2 13
RISK ANALYSIS FORMAT 13
    PURPOSE 13
    RISK-BASED ANALYSIS FORMAT 14
    NATURE OF BUSINESS 16
    RATINGS 16
    TRANSACTION / LIMIT DETAILS 17
    SECURITY / COLLATERAL 18
    DOCUMENTATION REQUIREMENTS & TERMS 20
    PARENTAL SUPPORT 21
    LOSS GIVEN DEFAULT ("LGD") % 22
    STOCK MARKET & 5-YEAR CDS SPREAD INFORMATION 22
    MANAGEMENT RISK 23
        Morality 23
    INTERNAL CONTROLS 24
    EXTERNAL REGULATION 25
    OTHER MACRO-ENVIRONMENTAL RISKS 25
    MICRO-ENVIRONMENTAL RISKS 27
    POTENTIAL CONCENTRATION & EVENT RISK 28
    FINANCIAL ANALYSIS 28

STRENGTHS & WEAKNESSES SUMMARY 29
CONCLUSION & RECOMMENDATION 29
IMPORTANT ISSUES IN ANALYSIS 29
   Relying On Information 29
   Using Up-To-Date Information 30
   Keeping Up-To-Date 31
   Credit Policy Breaches 31
Chapter 3 32
BASEL REGULATIONS FOR BANKS 32
CREDIT POLICY MANAGEMENT 32
BASEL I & II REGULATIONS 32
MINIMUM CAPITAL REQUIREMENT 33
   Standardised Approach: 33
   Internal Rating Based (IRB) Approach: 34
   Probability of Default ("PD"): 34
   Loss Given Default ("LGD"): 36
   BASEL III 40
   Capital Adequacy Requirement 40
   Additional Tier 1 Capital Ratio 40
   Leverage Ratio 41
   Liquidity Ratios 41
   Other Measures: 42
Chapter 4 44
FINANCIAL ANALYSIS OF BANKS 44
   SOVEREIGN STATE OWNERSHIP 44

EXTERNAL RATINGS REPORTS	44
THE BALANCE SHEET OF A BANK	45
Assets	45
Capital & Liabilities	47
THE INCOME STATEMENT OF A BANK	50
CASH FLOW STATEMENT	51
RATIOS & OTHER CREDIT METRICS	51
PROFITABILITY RATIOS	52
Return On Assets, Return on Risk-Weighted Assets & Return on Equity	52
Effective Tax Rate	53
Other Profitability Ratios	53
Net Interest Margin	53
Loan Loss Expense / Gross Interest Income (%)	54
REVENUE SPLIT	54
Operating Expenses / Net Revenue (%)	54
Net Lending Revenue / Net Revenue	54
PERSONNEL STATISTICS	55
Cost Per Employee	55
Net Revenue Per Employee	55
Employee Costs / Net Revenue	55
Employee Costs / Operating Expenses	56
LIQUIDITY RATIOS	56
Loans Made / Total Funding	56
Inter-Bank Borrowing / Loans Made	57

Adjusted Liquid Assets / Deposits Received 57

Liquid Assets + Deposits / Total Funding 58

Demand Deposits / Total Funding 58

Savings Deposits / Total Funding 58

Time Deposits / Total Funding 58

Interbank Borrowings / Total Funding 58

Other Borrowings / Total Funding 58

MATURITY PROFILES 59

ASSET QUALITY 60

Non-Performing Loans / Total Loans-Gross 61

Loan Loss Provision / Total Loans-Gross 62

Loan Loss Provisions / Non-Performing Loans 62

CAPITAL ADEQUACY 63

Risk-Weighted Assets / Total Assets & Contingents. 63

Total Capital / Risk-Weighted Assets 64

Tier 1 Capital / Risk-Weighted Assets 64

Tier 1 Capital / Total Capital 64

Total Capital / Net Loans Given 64

PROJECTIONS 65

PEER GROUP ANALYSIS 65

CONCLUSION REGARDING XYZ BANK'S FINANCIAL WELL-BEING 66

Chapter 5 67

ANALYZING NON-BANK FINANCIAL INSTITUTIONS 67

NON-BANK LENDING INSTITUTIONS 67

   BROKER-DEALERS / SECURITIES FIRMS 68

   INSURANCE COMPANIES 69

   FUNDS MANAGEMENT FIRMS & FUNDS 70

Chapter 6 74

ASSESSING OPERATIONAL RISK INTERNAL CONTROLS 74

Chapter 7 77

ASSESSING MARKET RISK INTERNAL CONTROLS 77

   OVERVIEW 77

   TYPES OF MARKET RISK 78

   MANAGEMENT OF MARKET RISK 79

   MARKET RISK CATEGORIES 79

   RISK MEASUREMENTS 80

   VALUE AT RISK ("VaR") 81

      Definition 81

      Monte Carlo Simulation 82

      Market Risk Factors 82

      Back-Testing 83

      Scenario & Stress Testing 84

   EXCESS MANAGEMENT 85

   PROPRIETARY TRADING BOOK LIMITS 86

      Securities Concentration 86

      Issuer Concentration 87

      Other Limits 87

Chapter 8 88

ASSESSING CREDIT RISK INTERNAL CONTROLS 88

THE BOARD OF DIRECTORS 88
DEFINITION OF CREDIT & COUNTERPARTY RISK 88
TYPES OF CREDIT & COUNTERPARTY RISK 89
    LENDING & CONTINGENT RISK 89
    ISSUER RISK 95
    UNDERWRITING RISK 95
    COUNTERPARTY RISK.. 96
    Financial Markets Division Set-Up 97
    Pre-Settlement Risk 100
    Pre-Settlement Risk Exposure Measurement 100
    Settlement Risk 102
    TRADE CREDIT GIVEN 104
    POLICYHOLDER RISK 104
"KNOW YOUR CUSTOMER ("KYC") & ACCOUNT OPENING REQUIREMENTS 105
NEW PRODUCTS 105
CREDIT RISK APPROVAL STRUCTURE 105
RESTRICTED & PROHIBITED ACTIVITIES 106
CREDIT RISK PORTFOLIO MANAGEMENT 106
CUSTOMER CONCENTRATION RISK 107
    CONTROLLING MAXIMUM EXPOSURE 107
    CREDIT LIMITS, OUTSTANDINGS & EXPOSURES 107
CREDIT RISK RATINGS 109
CREDIT RISK MITIGATION 110
    TRANSACTION STRUCTURE 110

  AVOIDING SUBORDINATION 110

  TAKING COLLATERAL / SECURITY 111

  LEGAL CLAUSES & FINANCIAL COVENANTS 114

  RECORDING RISK ON THIRD-PARTY GUARANTORS 115

 EXPOSURE MONITORING 115

  LIMIT EXCESSES & FAILED TRANSACTIONS 116

 PROBLEM CREDITS & WORK-OUTS 117

 COUNTRY RISK LIMITS 118

 REMUNERATION 119

 ROUND-UP 120

Chapter 9 121

CASE STUDY 1: LARGE BANK LTD. 121

 FINANCIAL STATEMENTS 133

Chapter 10 139

CASE STUDY 2: ABC HEDGE FUND 139

Chapter 1
INTRODUCTION BY THE AUTHOR

In my previous two books, I have explained how to analyze Corporates (industrial, manufacturing, retail and non-financial services firms), the focus being on operating cash flow analysis, and Insurance Companies, which are specialized financial institutions with their own "strange" terminology (to the layman), and incurred risks.

In this book, I explain how to analyze other financial institutions, including banks, funds and broker-dealers. Of paramount importance is understanding the Management team's strategy, which is a primary reason for financial institution failure. Examples of this are taking on securitization instruments (e.g. CDO investments) to diversify asset portfolio, but without understanding the risks and legal rights involved; diversifying into difficult geographical markets "at all costs" with insufficient local expertise, and weak asset funding, exacerbating asset-liability maturity mismatch. On top of this, we read about bank's mis-selling of financial services, including unemployment insurance in mortgage products; selling of highly-complex derivatives products to small firms, who don't really understand what they are getting themselves into, and manipulation of market rates, with hundreds of millions of dollars of regulatory fines for the industry. We also see how banks can be crippled by poor internal controls.

Financial institutions tend to be highly-regulated, particularly in developed markets, the notable exception being offshore hedge funds, where management is usually physically located in developed markets, but funds legally offshore. Hedge funds were originally investment vehicles aiming to "hedge" (i.e. reduce) risk, but now the focus in on achieving large returns with higher risk, the lower level of regulation permitting a wide variety of transactions, including short-selling. Investment in such vehicles is often set at a high level, with restrictions on marketing to the citizens of some countries, such as the United States. Compared to investments in mutual funds, unit trusts, investment trusts and pension funds, fees can be very high in total given additional performance incentives. Hedge funds have an advantage in being regarded as "alternative investments", having cash flows and returns which are not correlated to the usual investment categories of equity stocks, bonds, commodities, real estate property and precious metals. The reason for this is that they can invest in any assets; leverage highly (which means borrowing to finance asset purchases), and short-sell, fund Net Asset Value ("NAV") rising in price if securities fall in value, other things being equal. Understanding the hedge fund firm's strategy for managing funds is essential.

Whilst many financial institutions are covered by the external ratings agencies, independent analysis is always advisable if you are a decision-maker - You as an Analyst / Approver need to be confident on the decisions which you make or recommend, and you can only do this through your own analysis of information in the public domain, ratings reports being used as one source of information in this context.

This book explains how to assess financial institutions' financial well-being, Management capability and risk controls. There are also two case studies at the end, one for a multi-product bank, and the other for a hedge fund, to show how to put this into practice.

Chapter 2
RISK ANALYSIS FORMAT

PURPOSE

It is a good idea to have a structured approach in analyzing any organisation, this ensuring that you look at all appropriate aspects of proposed transactions, and do not miss out any important issues. A useful method is to use risk-based analysis, assessing transactional risk; quality of the Management team and internal controls; impact of external regulation and quality of this regulation; macro- and micro- environmental risks facing the firm, and the firm's financial well-being, which will (to a certain extent) reflect the afore-mentioned issues.

Two areas of particular importance are concentration risk and event risk. Although a firm may hitherto have a strong financial position, this may be owing to good market conditions, with a bit of luck thrown in, but the real test of a firm's strength is how it has coped, and will continue to cope, with difficult conditions, hence the importance of business diversification (which requires greater Management ability) and protection against / avoidance of one-off events, which might significantly damage business well-being.

RISK-BASED ANALYSIS FORMAT

A recommended format for analyzing financial institutions is as follows, with an explanation for each heading given below:

Customer Name & Nature of Business:

External Ratings:

Internal Rating:

Transaction / Limit Details:

Security / Collateral:

Documentation Requirements / Terms:

Parental Support

LGD % (For each facility):

Stock Market & Bond Spread Information:

Management Risk:

Internal Risk Controls:
- Operational Risks
- Market Risks
- Credit & Counterparty Risks

External Regulation:

Other Macro-Environmental Risks:
- Demographic
- Socio-Cultural
- Economic
- Technological
- Natural Environment
- Political and Country
- Legal Environmental
- Other

Micro-Environmental Risks (Competitive Environment):

Potential Concentration & Event Risks:

Financial Analysis:

Depending on the financial institution being analyzed, sub-headings might be:

- Balance Sheet
- Revenue
- Personnel Efficiency
- Profitability
- Liquidity & Funding
- Asset Quality
- Capital Adequacy
- Leverage

Strengths & Weaknesses Summary:

Conclusion & Recommendation:

NATURE OF BUSINESS

It is essential to understand the nature of the customer's business, and in which industry sector and geographical segments it operates, in order to assess its financial position and internal controls properly.

RATINGS

External agency reports and ratings can be very useful in determining the well-being of the firm being analyzed, but should be treated as one source of information, not an excuse for not doing your own work. Some organisations treat external ratings in this way, viewing additional work as a "waste of time if the experts have already done it". However, my view is that it is not an Analyst's job to be a "cut and paster", but to undertake an expert independent assessment of available information. Also, doing your own analysis helps you to understand whether statements made in ratings and broker reports are accurate, giving you an impetus to look deeper if there are differences of opinion.

Financial institutions have their own internal rating methodology and systems, using quantitative and qualitative information to derive a rating and probability of default range. It is recommended that external ratings should be used as a cap on internal rating. So, if the internal rating generated by your system is better than the external rating, it would be prudent to override your internal rating to that of the external rating equivalent.

However, if the internal rating is worse than the external rating, leave it as it is.

Further information on ratings is provided in the later chapter of this book on Credit Risk Internal Controls.

TRANSACTION / LIMIT DETAILS

It is important to understand the nature of the transactional risk being proposed, whether it be a direct investment in the financial institution's equity stock, or provision of credit limits in the form of short-term deposits; other direct lending, such as participation in syndicated lending; derivatives; stock borrowing & lending transactions; repos / reverse repos; securities trading or trade finance risk.

Of key importance other than transaction nature, is the proposed amount of the risk, its term / tenor (being the contractual length of time the risk is held), and how it will change during this period. As a general rule, the longer the transaction, the greater the risk, so a 5-year loan participation will be more risky than a short-term (i.e. <= 1 year) loan, other things being equal. And, depending on the transaction, the risk amount may actually reduce over the term of the contract, so an amortizing loan, namely one where repayment of principal amount is made periodically during the loan, will be less risky than one of same initial amount with a bullet (i.e. single) repayment at the end. Likewise, in looking at derivative trades, it is important to look at the trade profile, namely how maximum potential future exposure ("PFE"){the estimated replacement cost of the contract if there is a default situation} changes over the life of the trade, this being different depending on the nature of the underlying instrument, whether it be interest rates, FX rates, equities prices or commodity prices.

An important issue is to clearly understand the purpose of the proposed business, and whether it is reasonable in the context of the customer's business.

SECURITY / COLLATERAL

In this respect, a distinction is made between tangible security, which relates to assets (mainly illiquid) used to secure Banking Book products, and eligible collateral used to secure Trading Book products. For Banking Book risks, such as loans and trade finance, booked exposure amount is not impacted by the value of security. An example would be a mortgage loan to a medium-sized broker with a view to its purchase of a commercial property. If the loan is for USD 5 million, and the securing property is worth USD 6 million, the risk amount is still shown as USD 5 million in the Banking Book. However, if the broker has a USD 5 million derivatives limit, documented via ISDA, and a Credit Support Annex ("CSA") with threshold amount of USD 1 million, the limit amount will be set at somewhere above USD 1 million, not USD 5 million. This is owing to the fact that the value of eligible collateral (mainly cash and liquid securities) held by the derivative provider can be deducted from the maximum PFE amount of the relevant trades in determining utilization level. The CSA threshold amount of USD 1 million represents the amount of uncollateralized risk the derivative provider is willing to accept in total before a margin call is made (i.e. the customer is approached to provide additional collateral). Theoretically, the customer could default just after the margin call is made, meaning that the derivative provider's uncollateralized risk is USD 1 million plus any negative market movements during the close-out period, which is often set at 14 days. Hence why the limit will be set at above USD 1 million.

Some transactions are inherently secured / collateralized, being termed "self-securing", examples being (i) stock borrowing & lending (relating to lending of cash against securities, with relevant haircut/margin - usually around 5% of liquid assets, meaning that for every USD 100 of securities, USD 95 cash will be lent); (ii) repos / reverse repos (which have the same economic effect as the aforementioned, with the technical difference that the "cash lender" actually owns the securities received as collateral, but is legally required to resell them back to the "cash borrower" at maturity; (iii) certain trade finance products where the underlying traded goods are held as security, and (iv) leases, finance leases equating to loans secured by the assets leased (technically remaining the property of the lessor / lender, and being on-balance sheet, and operating leases being off-balance sheet rental contracts, but with the same economic effect as finance leases, being treated as "quasi debt".

To avoid operational risk associated with enforcing security / collateral in a default situation, it is important that documentation is written and executed under correct procedures, usually involving the bank's internal legal department and, where appropriate, external counsel. I have personally seen cases where security / collateral documentation has not been executed correctly, or has been lost, leading to the risk-taker's inability to enforce.

On this subject, a few years' ago, many top banks got involved in diversifying their books by purchasing collateralized debt obligation ("CDO") tranches, which are securitized portfolios of credit assets. A certain variety of these had underlying portfolio investments in sub-prime mortgages, being low-quality mortgage loans. When many of these loans went bad, the banks holding the CDOs attempted to enforce the mortgage security, but were found in court to be incapable of doing this since they did not have access to the underlying security documentation. Whilst their purchase of the CDOs had given them an economic right to the underlying cash flows from the mortgage lending, it did not give them a legal right to sell the properties mortgaged!! This situation led to many banks having to write-off millions of dollars of their investment, leading to a banking crisis and need for bolstered capital adequacy regulations and supervision.

DOCUMENTATION REQUIREMENTS & TERMS

This section of your analysis should cover the nature of the documentation (e.g. a facility letter / loan agreement for direct lending; ISDA / CSA for derivatives; Terms of Business letter for securities cash trading; OSLA / GESLA for stock borrowing and lending; MRA / GMRA for repos and reverse repos, etc.), together with important terms. As an example, for direct lending, financial covenants and cross-default measures will be important. For derivatives trading, important clauses are cross-default / acceleration (giving the ability to close-out trades above a certain threshold amount if the firm has defaulted on facilities with third-parties - but only if the third party has started legal proceedings in the case of acceleration); external ratings downgrade (termination is permitted if the external ratings fall below an agreed level), and CSA threshold amount (stating agreed uncollateralized level of risk), as well as initial margin ("independent amount") and minimum transfer amount (to avoid the nuisance of transferring insignificant sums).

PARENTAL SUPPORT

In transacting with a separate legal entity within a wider customer Group, there is the potential for loss to be incurred if the legal entity is weak and the parent Group fails to help it. This is unlikely for core and strategic companies, but may occur for non-core companies expected to be divested. Obtaining a parental guarantee, which legally obliges the parent to repay the debt, and/or other stated liabilities, in a subsidiary default situation, effectively shifts the risk to the parent, so rating would be calculated based on the parent. For lower levels of support, such as a Letter of Comfort or verbal assurances from senior management, such a shifting is not possible, but may provide comfort to the Analyst that the parent will not allow the subsidiary to default.

LOSS GIVEN DEFAULT ("LGD") %

This is a measure used to calculate capital adequacy under Basel regulations (see later chapter), and is often calculated by professional Credit Analysts for the banks where they work. The practice is for every credit facility to be assigned an LGD% using system-based models, this impacting the pricing of such facilities. It is not a risk analysis requirement as such, but more of a revenue / profitability criterion used by banks to ensure that the business which they are undertaking will be profitable, other things being equal. Please refer to the description of RAROC measure later in this book.

STOCK MARKET & 5-YEAR CDS SPREAD INFORMATION

This information is used to gauge Market perception of the company. If it is quoted, share price data will be available, including current share price; where this sits within the 12-month range (showing the strength of current Market view); market capitalisation (shares issued x share price, being the market value of the company), and beta (share price volatility relative to the Market, a number greater than 1 showing higher volatility, and a number below one showing lower volatility.

The 5-year Credit Default Swap spread, and how it has increased or decreased, also shows the perceived riskiness of the customer.

MANAGEMENT RISK

As with any organisation, it is essential for it to be led by a top quality management team, and for no single person to have so much power that he / she could destroy a solid business through incorrect decisions. Excellent Corporate Governance is essential, this normally involving a highly skilled and experienced Board of Executive and Non-Executive directors, being led by a Chairman, with a separate Chief Executive Officer ("CEO") responsible for running the business. It was quite common a few years' ago for the Chairman and CEO to be a single person, but this had the tendency to allow poor decisions to creep in, sometimes leading to significant losses. Splitting these roles allows an additional safeguard to poor personal decisions. Indeed, poor Management decisions is the key reason why banks have lost their good reputation in recent years, those such as CDO investments previously mentioned, having big repercussions, not only for the banking industry, but for world economies in general.

Morality

The banking industry is essential to commercial success, and therefore to the success of whole economies. It also has a big political influence, financing a whole variety of industries, from supermarkets to defence companies. Senior management of banks, and indeed lower-level employees, and those of commercial enterprises, therefore have personal responsibility for ensuring that the money which their organisation lends or borrows is used for wholesome and moral purposes. In the past, the banking industry has financed wars, and to this day, finances companies which produce items designed to intentionally harm people. In my experience, the bank Relationship and Credit Officers, who put forward and approve lending for such companies, are not bad people, but somehow, in their minds, separate their job from their personal values and morals. For me, "morality" means pretty much doing what you want, provided that you do not intentionally cause harm to yourself or others. As a Credit Officer, I could never sacrifice this by hiding behind my job. You cannot separate yourself from your work decisions. Banks will often have a "Transactional Committee", which looks at reputational issues for the bank, but this is not the same as morality. What is needed generally, in both banking and the business world, is good decision-making based on morality, avoiding products which cause harm to other living things.

INTERNAL CONTROLS

This is very much linked to the quality of the financial institution's Management team, poor internal controls naturally resulting in losses and possible eventual insolvency over time. The main categories of risk management policies, procedures and processes are (i) Operational Risk; (ii) Market Risk, and (iii) Credit Risk, these being covered in separate chapters of this book.

EXTERNAL REGULATION

This is very important for financial institutions, the higher the quality of regulation and control, the more likely that the organisation will remain solvent. Each division of the bank, in liaison with its Compliance department, will ensure that it has policies and procedures which meet regulatory requirements and that they are met, Internal Audit periodically checking this. In most developed markets, it is generally safe to assume that financial institutions operating within them are following the regulations, but there may be less certainty in lesser-developed markets, it therefore being more important that internal controls are looked at carefully, and security / collateral taken as appropriate.

OTHER MACRO-ENVIRONMENTAL RISKS

Other Macro-Environmental Risk categories are (i) Demographic; (ii) Socio-Cultural; (iii) Economic; (iv) Technological; (v) Natural Environment ; (vi) Political / Country, (vi) Legal and (vii) Other, including the effect of terrorist attacks.

A financial institution will be impacted by demographic issues, including how to market wealthy segments of the population (usually older), who have greater investment and savings power; provide loans to the poorer segments, and cater for the needs of those at certain stages of their life (e.g. needing accommodation - mortgage loans, or specific assets - personal loans, HP agreements, or other financing arrangements).

Socio-cultural issues will be important in terms of what is considered suitable behaviour. Some markets, for example, prefer property ownership and others renting; some prefer car ownership, and others, public transport. Some cultures would rather keep their money in physical assets, being sceptical of banks and "intangible" investments, and others prefer the safety of a bank.

Economic factors influence customers' willingness to invest in certain types of product, current very low interest rates making investors think twice about whether to tie-up their money in longer-term savings accounts, and borrowers buying larger or better assets given largely immaterial financing costs.

Technological advances have both reduced employment costs and increased operating risks through fraud and system break-downs.

Natural environmental issues can generally impact locally-based organisations more than global ones, examples being the impact of bad weather conditions (e.g. hurricanes) and other so-called "Acts of God", including floods, tsunamis, earthquakes and even Sun-spot activity, which can take-out electricity supplies for months! The potential for such risks, and adequacy of insurance cover, should be established.

Political and country risks can have a major impact on financial institution customers, particularly if the firm is based in a particularly volatile region. If these are viewed as particularly high risk, suitable collateral should be taken (held in a stable country, ideally yours).

Legal risks include the ability of your customer to own assets in a country, and difficulties in enforcing security.

Other risks include the effect of terrorist action on operations, an example being the WTC disaster, which effectively wiped out a number of banks and securities firms, whose operations were concentrated in that area.

MICRO-ENVIRONMENTAL RISKS

This heading relates to the competitive environment in which the financial institution operates, its relative strengths and weaknesses being determined by (i) the bargaining power of customers, which will be high for large multinationals; (ii) bargaining power of suppliers, which effectively refers to depositors and other providers of funds to banks, which will largely be related to economic factors, such as interest rates; (iii) threat of entry into the financial institution's existing segments by new operators; (iv) threat of substitutes, such as on-line products rather than branch-based ones, and (v) ability to compete with existing financial institutions, such as providing higher rates to depositors, lower rates for borrowers, and lower fees and better services for other customers, relative to competitors.

POTENTIAL CONCENTRATION & EVENT RISK

This is very much linked to internal risk controls, and ability to obtain insurance for significant event risks, such as terrorist attacks.

FINANCIAL ANALYSIS

This is covered more fully in a later chapter, but will cover such areas as balance sheet structure; asset quality; liquidity and funding; capital adequacy; leverage (i.e. borrowing level, particularly important for funds); revenue generation; efficiency of staff; peer group analysis, and forecasts / projections. Financial analysis is usually undertaken primarily on the Group, using the consolidated financial statements of the parent, with a brief analysis on each legal entity within the Group for which there is exposure. So, if we intend to lend to ABC Limited, which is a wholly-owned subsidiary of DEF plc, we would undertake primary analysis on DEF's consolidated financials, also summarising ABC's financial well-being within this wider Group. For funds, you will analyze the well-being of the fund, unless transactional risk is very low, and it is agreed that the asset management firm's financial position will be looked at instead. - This is often the case for low-risk DVP cash securities trading where the asset management firm is acting as agent on behalf of a large number of underlying funds as principals.

The key issue is determining whether the customer will continue to have a satisfactory financial position during the term of our exposure, and be able to meet its obligations without difficulty.

STRENGTHS & WEAKNESSES SUMMARY

This is a summary of all the good and bad points regarding the financial institution's well-being as covered in the above sections, and will be the basis of your conclusions about the firm, and your recommendation / decision on whether the proposed transaction is acceptable.

CONCLUSION & RECOMMENDATION

This gives your overall view of the financial institution's well-being, leading into your recommendation on whether, and how, to progress with the proposed business.

IMPORTANT ISSUES IN ANALYSIS

Relying On Information

Although there have been one or two exceptions in the not too distant past, financial statements audited by a major accountancy firm can generally be relied upon as being accurate.   Interim figures, which have been reviewed, but not fully audited, are also generally acceptable, but figures produced by the firm, without any independent check, must be treated with caution. For major financial institutions, they are probably fine given sophistication of processes and need for Management to ensure accurate release of information to avoid prosecution under stock exchange and other regulations. Caution is needed in assessing information supplied by smaller, unquoted entities.

Using Up-To-Date Information

In analyzing any company, you must use the most up-to-date information available and, if the information which you have is too old or irrelevant, it would be wise to defer a decision until up-to-date information is available. Quoted financial institutions will publish their annual report a few months after the financial year-end date, usually within 3-6 months. They also publish unaudited (but reviewed) interim figures either every quarter or half-year. Information on forecasts / projections may be available, often provided in Analysts' conference calls and broker reports, but Management has to be very careful on what information is released since this will be of a price-sensitive nature; i.e. impact the share price. Private information (i.e. not in the public domain) must never be used to buy or sell shares, this being illegal "insider dealing". This is the reason why banks and other financial institutions have "Chinese Walls" or "Information Barriers" within their organisations to ensure that potentially price-sensitive information, or views held by

Relationship Management and Credit staff, are kept away from trading staff.

For unquoted, private firms, such as some fund managers, it may be possible and necessary to obtain internally-produced financial statements and forecasts if there is little information in the public domain. In using such information, it is important to understand that forecasts are likely to be optimistic unless independently audited / reviewed.

Keeping Up-To-Date

Once exposure has been put on the books, Analysts need to keep up-to-date with developments, reading the press; using ratings agency alerts, and undertaking periodic reviews (at least annually).

Credit Policy Breaches

These will generally not be agreed, but if a potential breach is considered acceptable, this should clearly be stated within the analysis, and usually discussed with senior management beforehand to gauge reasonable likelihood of agreement.

Chapter 3
BASEL REGULATIONS FOR BANKS

CREDIT POLICY MANAGEMENT

If you are a professional Credit Officer, you will appreciate how important it is to keep up to date with regulations in your particular industry sector, both local and international. For larger organisations, there will usually be a Credit Policy Officer, with responsibility for this, and suggesting any changes to internal policy to a senior Committee for approval, and circulation to appropriate officers.

Your organisation's policy and procedures documents should contain full information on how to handle requests for business involving credit exposure, the main areas being similar to the contents of this book. Different banks, for example, have different specific ways of doing things based on their size and products on offer, but all will have a similar approach owing to international banking regulations.

BASEL I & II REGULATIONS

I shall provide a brief summary of the key aspects of the Basel Committee on Banking Supervision regulations, the implications of these on internal risk management being covered in the various chapters of this book. Obviously, as regulations change, internal policies, procedures and practices need to change to accommodate these. The Three Pillars set out the requirements needed by a bank to ensure that its capital base is sufficient, and operations properly managed, these being: (i) The Minimum Capital Requirement; (ii) Supervisory Review Process, and (iii) Market Discipline.

MINIMUM CAPITAL REQUIREMENT

In order for a bank to meet this requirement, its Capital Ratio, as defined below, must be 8% or better:

Bank's Capital Ratio = Total Capital / Risk Weighted Assets x 100 (%)

where Risk Weighted Assets are quantified as Credit Risk + Market Risk + Operational Risk

There are two alternative approaches used, the Advanced Approach (for larger, more sophisticated banks), and the Standardised Approach (for smaller banks). For the former, data integrity in relation to Probability of Default (on which internal rating is based) and Loss Given Default (on which pricing is calculated) is essential.

Standardised Approach:

The bank allocates a standard risk-weighting to each of its assets, and off-balance sheet positions, to derive a sum of risk-weighted asset values. A risk weight of 100 % means that an exposure is included in the calculation of risk-weighted assets at its full value, which translates into a capital charge equal to 8 percent of that value. Similarly, a risk weight of 20 % results in a capital charge of 1.6 percent (0.2 x 8). Individual risk weightings are determined by reference to a standardised list, there being four categories (20 %, 50 %, 100 % and 150 %) depending on the nature and external rating of the counterparty.

Internal Rating Based (IRB) Approach:

There are four risk components within the IRB approach for corporate, bank and sovereign exposures, which build off the structure of banks' rating systems. These are: (i) Probability of Default (PD) of a borrower, which is related to the internal rating given to the customer / counterparty. (ii) Loss Given Default (LGD) of a transaction, which determines pricing. (iii) Exposure At Default (EAD) of a transaction. (iv) Maturity (M) of the transaction.

Probability of Default ("PD"):

The core of the IRB approach is the use of banks' own estimates of the probability of default (PD) associated with an exposure. The bank will have its own internal rating methodology, sometimes influenced by external agency ratings, whereby quantitative and qualitative information derived from credit analysis of the customer / counterparty is input into the bank's rating system and an internal rating produced. If this is materially different to the external rating, it is quite common (but not always) for the system-derived rating to be overridden. The choice as to whether or not to do this depends on the Credit Officer's confidence that the external ratings are more accurate based on current information. If there is such confidence, the weakest of the external ratings is often used as the official rating. Some banks prefer not to override internally-generated ratings at all, based on the argument that this upsets the calibration of the system.

Under banks' credit policy, each rating is assigned a PD range based on the industry sector in which the customer / counterparty operates. So, once the rating has been calculated for the particular customer, the bank knows the quantified likelihood that it will default within a 1-year timeframe, which is very low for better-rated entities. Given the short timeframe of the PD, banks will undertake a credit analysis review of each customer / counterparty at least once a year.

In deriving the PD range for each internal rating, the bank can use a variety of sources of information, including data based on the bank's own default experience; mapping to external data, and / or use of statistical default models. Whatever is chosen, estimates should represent a realistic view of the long-term average of the probability of default associated with borrowers in each rating.

In the IRB approach, there are two ways to recognise credit risk mitigation in the form of obtained guarantees (e.g. from a parent), and purchased guarantees and credit derivatives from third parties: (i) A Foundation Approach, which is based on substitution with a capital floor element. (ii) Advanced Approach, which uses a "substitution ceiling", whereby a bank would base its capital calculation on the borrower rating of the underlying obligor, adjusted to reflect the effect of the guarantee. This "notching" would not be allowed to go beyond the higher of the borrower or guarantor ratings (i.e. no more favourable than full substitution).

Loss Given Default ("LGD"):

Otherwise known as "Severity", this is required for each corporate exposure, being a measure of the expected average loss that the bank will experience per unit of exposure should the counterparty default. Unlike PD, where a borrower can have only one rating (and thus one PD), different product exposures to that borrower may have different LGD profiles given facility-specific features. There are essentially two approaches, the one to use depending on the bank's size and level of sophistication:

- Foundation Approach:

Estimates of LGD are provided according to standardised supervisory parameters, using a relatively simple categorisation of exposures according to whether the loan is senior or subordinated and whether, and to what extent, certain restricted forms of collateral have been taken. In terms of "subordination", there are essentially two varieties: (i) Legal Subordination, where the facility is subordinated to other financiers' credit exposures; e.g. a junior participation in a leveraged syndicated lending facility will legally be repaid after senior lenders. (ii) Structural Subordination, where financiers to other corporate entities in the customer / counterparty Group have prior rights over our lending to a particular entity; e.g. We lend to a non-operating company, but other financiers lend to the main operating companies. The risk in the latter case arises owing to the likelihood that a non-operating company will have fewer assets and income than an operating one, so if the Group goes into insolvency, lenders to the operating company will have access to greater liquidation monies owing to insolvency rules. Under the Foundation Approach unsecured exposure gives an LGD of 50% for senior claims on corporates, and 75 % for subordinated claims. Generally lower LGDs are applied where there is tangible security (e.g. real estate property) or eligible collateral for traded product exposures (e.g. derivatives with an ISDA / CSA):

- **Advanced Approach:**

Those banks, which demonstrate that their estimates of LGD are suitably robust, are permitted to use them. The advantages are: (i) A wider range of LGD categories. (ii) This will recognise the bank's own loss experience. (iii) The bank's internal practices (products offered, lending practices, recovery procedures, etc.) which can have a material impact on LGD, will be recognised. (iv) Important differences in lending standards and legal environments across markets and products can be recognised. (v) A wider range of collateral is permitted.

Exposure at Default ("EAD")

For on-balance sheet transactions, EAD is identical to the nominal amount of exposure. On-balance sheet netting of loans and deposits is permitted to reduce the estimate of EAD. For off-balance sheet items, a broader approach is adopted:

A. Transactions with an uncertain future drawdown (e.g. commitments and revolving credits)

- Foundation Approach: 75 % of the off-balance sheet amount. Where a facility comprises both a drawn amount and an undrawn amount, EAD will be calculated as 100 % of the drawn amount plus 75 % of the undrawn balance. There are other credit conversion factors ("CCF") for other off-balance sheet items: e.g. (i) Guarantees / standby letters of credit / acceptances: 100 % CCF; (ii) performance / bid bonds, standby L/Cs related to specific transactions: 50 % CCF; (iii) self-liquidating contingencies (e.g. L/Cs secured by shipments): 20 % CCF; (iv) sale and repurchase agreements / assets sales with recourse: 100 % CFF; (v) forward asset purchases, etc.: 100 % CCF; (vi) note issuances / revolving underwriting facilities: 50 % CCF. If the Advanced Approach is used, internal estimates of EAD are permitted subject to demonstration of minimum requirements.

B. Over-The-Counter ("OTC") forex, interest rate and equity derivative contracts. ("OTC" means sale of derivatives directly rather than through an Exchange).

- Credit risk equivalent amounts on these contracts are measured as the sum of the replacement cost (positive mark-to-market) of the transaction plus specified "add-ons" (which vary by transaction type and residual maturity) to reflect potential future exposure (PFE). Add-ons range from 0 to 15 percent of the notional amount. Under the Advanced approach, sophisticated banks are permitted to use their own estimates. All estimates of EAD are net of any specific provisions a bank may have raised against an exposure.

Maturity

Maturity is a key factor affecting the risk of a credit product. Banks recognise the importance of maturity as a driver of risk through their pricing; in their internal assessments of capital adequacy, and in performance measurement reviews, such as RAROC (Risk Adjusted Return on Capital). Bank credit policies impose tougher internal requirements on longer maturity loans, and indeed limits on maturity, depending on the perceived strength of the customer.

Under the Foundation Approach, all exposures can be treated as having the same conservative assessment of average maturity of 3 years. In this case, risk weighting an exposure would depend only on its PD and LGD. Under the Advanced Approach, the bank would be required to explicitly incorporate maturity effects on risk weights. As such, a credit exposure's risk weight would depend on its PD, LGD and "effective maturity", which emphasises the contractual rather than economic maturity of exposures. The Effective Maturity (1 year minimum, capped at 7 years max) is the maximum remaining time in years that the borrower could take to repay.

BASEL III

Basel III provides additional capital adequacy requirements to the afore-mentioned rules, with some amendments.

Capital Adequacy Requirement

The requirement for the bank's Capital Ratio remains at 8%, being calculated as Total Capital (Tier 1- core capital + Tier 2-supplementary capital) / Risk Weighted Assets x 100 (%). Tier 3 has been abolished.

Additional Tier 1 Capital Ratio

The predominant form of Tier 1 capital must be common shares and retained earnings. Since 2015, a minimum Tier 1 (CET1) ratio of 4.5% must be maintained at all times by a bank. There are also two additional capital buffers: (i) A mandatory "capital conservation buffer", equivalent to 2.5% of risk-weighted assets. With the 4.5% CET1 capital ratio required, banks have to hold a total of 7% CET1 capital, from 2019 onwards. (ii) A "discretionary counter-cyclical buffer", allowing national regulators to require additional capital during periods of high credit growth, the level of this buffer being between 0% and 2.5% of RWA, and must be met by CET1 capital.

As of September 2010, proposed Basel III norms sought ratios as: 7–9.5% (4.5% + 2.5% (conservation buffer) + 0–2.5% (seasonal buffer)) for common equity; 8.5–11% for Tier 1 capital, and 10.5–13% for total capital.

Leverage Ratio

Basel III has also introduced a minimum "leverage ratio" of 3% minimum, this being increased by local central banks as desired. In July 2013, for example, the U.S. Federal Reserve announced that the minimum leverage ratio would be 6% for eight systemically-important banks, and 5% for their insured bank holding companies. The leverage ratio is a non-risk-based leverage ratio, calculated by dividing Tier 1 capital by the bank's average total consolidated assets (sum of the exposures of all assets and non-balance sheet items).

Liquidity Ratios

Basel III introduced two required liquidity ratios: (i) The Liquidity Coverage Ratio ("LCR"), requiring a bank to hold sufficient high-quality liquid assets to cover its total net cash outflows over 30 days. (ii) The Net Stable Funding Ratio, requiring the available amount of stable funding to exceed the required amount of stable funding over a one-year period of extended stress.

In October 2013, the US Federal Reserve proposed that financial institutions, and FSOC-designated non-bank financial companies, should have an adequate stock of high-quality liquid assets ("HQLA") that can be quickly liquidated to meet liquidity needs over a short period of time. The LCR numerator is the value of HQLA, and the denominator is the total net cash outflows over a specified stress period (total expected cash outflows minus total expected cash inflows). Large Bank Holding Companies ("BHCs"), with over USD 250 billion in consolidated assets, should hold enough HQLA (a haircut applied based on asset quality) to cover 30 days of net cash outflow. Regional firms, with USD 50-250 billion of assets, would need to hold enough HQLA to cover 21 days of net cash outflow. Smaller BHCs, those with under USD 50 billion, would remain subject to the prevailing qualitative supervisory framework. The proposal requires that the LCR be at least equal to (or greater than) 1.0, and includes a multi-year transition period that would require: 80% compliance starting 1 January 2015, 90% compliance starting 1 January 2016, and 100% compliance starting 1 January 2017.

Other Measures:

A series of measures is to be introduced to promote the build-up of capital buffers in good times, that can be drawn upon in periods of stress. Banks will be required to produce more forward looking provisions, conducting stress tests that include widening credit spreads in recessionary scenarios. Also, the aim is to change accounting standards towards an expected loss ("EL") approach, whereby EL amount = LGD x PD x EAD.

Chapter 4
FINANCIAL ANALYSIS OF BANKS

SOVEREIGN STATE OWNERSHIP

If an emerging market, or indeed developed market, bank is owned by a Sovereign State, and there is reason to suppose that the bank is integral to that State (e.g. with provision of a guarantee, or clear supportive intent), financial analysis of the bank is somewhat secondary to the well-being of the Sovereign State. The internal rating will be aligned to that of the State (where guaranteed), or its standalone rating notched upwards and capped at that level.

The assumption in this chapter is that the bank is an essentially independent, standalone entity, not supported by third parties. Analysis of the bank Group's financial well-being therefore becomes essential, along with macro- and micro- environmental issues.

EXTERNAL RATINGS REPORTS

The external ratings agencies do an excellent job in analyzing the financial and business risks of many financial institutions, providing a rating which aligns to a probability of default range. Indeed, most professional risk analysts working for banks and other organisations subscribe to at least one of these agencies' report services. However, not all financial institutions, including emerging market banks, are externally-rated, and information may now be available which is not covered in the latest report, meaning that Risk Analysts need to be able to do their own analysis. Also, many organisations require their Analysts to come to their own view on the financial institution's well-being and rating, using the external rating report effectively as a check, rather than the primary information source. Analysts therefore need to understand how to analyze financial institutions correctly, not only for their own report-writing purposes, but also to understand assessments provided by third parties.

THE BALANCE SHEET OF A BANK

I shall provide below an explanation of the most important components of the bank's financial statements, by reference to a fictional bank, XYZ Bank (based on a real one), in the context of a request to our Credit Department to deposit funds up to USD 50 million with that bank.

Assets

A bank's assets consist mainly of loans given to customers, and liquid assets needed to meet commitments as they fall due, mainly operating outflows and repayments to depositors.

BANK ANALYZED: XYZ BANK

BALANCE SHEET	31/12/X1	31/12/X2	31/12/X3	
Currency:	USD K	USD K	USD K	
Denomination:	1,000	1,000	1,000	

ASSETS

Cash & Equivalents	16,249,890	6,478,201	5,801,459	4.0%
Government Securities	103,806,539	28,228,975	20,417,590	14.2%
Quoted Bonds				
Quoted Equities				
LIQUID ASSETS	**120,056,429**	**34,707,176**	**26,219,049**	**18.2%**
Deposits with Central Banks	17,080,000	18,830,000	5,422,000	3.8%
Deposits with Local banks	462,570	105	8,621	0.0%
Deposits with Other banks	24,330,490	15,202,924	17,068,256	11.8%
TOTAL DEPOSITS MADE	**41,873,060**	**34,033,029**	**22,498,877**	**15.6%**
Loans Made - Gross	91,419,069	67,180,104	45,203,405	31.4%
Less: Loan Loss Provisions	-3,481,365	-2,143,936	-1,522,117	-1.1%
LOANS MADE - NET	**87,937,704**	**65,036,168**	**43,681,288**	**30.3%**
TOTAL DEP + LOANS	**129,810,764**	**99,069,197**	**66,180,165**	**45.9%**
Derivative Financial Instruments				
Other Operating Assets	16,215,035	16,593,043	15,788,347	11.0%
TOT. OTHER OP. ASSETS	**16,215,035**	**16,593,043**	**15,788,347**	**11.0%**
Restricted Funds	14,644,918	5,781,936	2,561,232	1.8%
Available For Sale Investments				
TOTAL OTHER ASSETS	**14,644,918**	**5,781,936**	**2,561,232**	**1.8%**
Unconsolidated Subs. & Assoc.	3,557,734	1,746,213	1,617,206	1.1%
Property, Plant & Equipment	11,729,436	7,399,936	4,022,808	2.8%
Other Fixed Assets	9,066,250	2,600,203	3,309,433	2.3%
Goodwill & Other Intangible Assets				
TOTAL LT ASSETS	**24,353,420**	**11,746,352**	**8,949,447**	**6.2%**
TOTAL B/S ASSETS	**305,080,566**	**167,897,704**	**119,698,240**	**83.1%**
	62,347,504	46,231,831	24,375,155	16.9%
TOTAL CONTINGENT ASSETS (See Contingent Liabs)				
TOTAL ASSETS & CONTINGENTS	**367,428,070**	**214,129,535**	**144,073,395**	**100.0%**

In this example, XYZ Bank's balance sheet has significantly reduced in size, falling from total balance sheet assets of USD 305.1 billion in 20X1 to around a third of that (USD 119.7 billion) in 20X3. Loans made have reduced materially, as have liquid asset level, investments and PP&E. Contingent assets have also reduced materially. The reason for this is that XYZ Bank sold off some of its key businesses in 20X2/X3 as a means of focusing its activities on what it saw as its core business.

Capital & Liabilities

The Liabilities side of the balance sheet consists predominantly of deposits received from customers, and borrowings from the inter-bank market and elsewhere, these funds being used to on-lend to customers. Retail (i.e. personal) customer deposits are considered to be much more stable than inter-bank borrowings, even if they can be legally withdrawn at short notice. Banks in general have what is known as an "asset-liability maturity mismatch" in that loans given to borrowing customers tend to be of a longer-term nature (mortgage loans being particularly long), but deposits received and inter-bank borrowings used to fund these, being of a much shorter legal period. A bank could experience a serious liquidity problem if there is an unusually high withdrawal of deposits - An example of this is when a bank is reported to be in trouble, leading to a "run on the bank", whereby customers look to get their monies out "before the bank collapses". This is the reason why Basel III aims to ensure that banks have adequate liquidity to meet deposit repayments, and other regulations require some of their liquid assets to be held at the central bank.

Tier 1 and 2 capital also represent major items on the Liabilities side of the balance sheet, Basel regulations requiring certain minimum levels to be kept, as described in the last chapter.

Contingent liabilities are off-balance sheet, but can be added-in on both the Assets and Liabilities sides of the balance sheet for analytical purposes, to gain a clear picture of their relative size. Examples are potential commitments under (i) acceptance of bills of exchange and notes, whereby the bank guarantees payment if the primary obligor fails to pay; (ii) guarantees and performance bond commitments, whereby the bank pays the recipient if the primary obligor or contractor fails to honour its commitments, and (iii) self-liquidating contingencies, generally of a short-term nature.

	31/12/X1 USD K	31/12/X2 USD K	31/12/X3 USD K	
CAPITAL & LIABILITIES				
Share Capital	3,000,000	3,000,000	2,000,000	1.4%
Other Non-Distributable Reserves	32,215,695	29,046,318	8,327,013	5.8%
Retained Earnings Reserve	1,229,847	1,421,718	1,290,965	0.9%
	36,445,542	33,468,036	11,617,978	8.1%
TIER 1 CAPITAL (CORE CAPITAL)				
Redeemable Preference Shares				
Other LT Capital Items	9,237,585	6,909,788	3,525,804	2.4%
TIER 2 CAPITAL	9,237,585	6,909,788	3,525,804	2.4%
TOTAL CAPITAL	45,683,127	40,377,824	15,143,782	10.5%
Demand Deposits Received	106,423,781	61,017,727	55,909,590	38.8%
Savings Deposits Received	7,289,209	3,301,591	1,664,875	1.2%
Time Deposits Received	108,306,490	39,688,073	24,929,457	17.3%

Inter-Bank Borrowings	105,000	930,164	949,255	0.7%
CORE FUNDING	**222,124,480**	**104,937,555**	**83,453,177**	**57.9%**
Debt Securities Issued				
Repos & Similar Borrowings				
Other Borrowings	25,255,771	15,660,361	17,012,007	11.8%
OTHER BORROWINGS	**25,255,771**	**15,660,361**	**17,012,007**	**11.8%**
TOTAL FUNDING	**247,380,251**	**120,597,916**	**100,465,184**	**69.7%**
Derivatives				
Other Liabilities	12,017,188	6,921,964	4,089,274	2.8%
TOTAL OTHER LIABILITIES	**12,017,188**	**6,921,964**	**4,089,274**	**2.8%**
TOTAL CAPITAL & LIABILITIES	**305,080,566**	**167,897,704**	**119,698,240**	**83.1%**
Contingent Liabilities				
Acceptances & Performance Guarantees Issued	62,286,654	46,231,831	24,375,155	16.9%
Securing Guarantees Issued				
L/Cs & Other Trade Contingents	60,850			
TOTAL CONTINGENT LIABILITIES	**62,347,504**	**46,231,831**	**24,375,155**	**16.9%**
TOTAL CAPITAL, LIABILITIES & CONTINGENTS	**367,428,070**	**214,129,535**	**144,073,395**	**100.0%**

As a result of the Group's restructuring, XYX Bank's capital base fell materially, Tier 1 falling from USD 36.5 billion in 20X1 to USD 11.6 billion in 20X3, Tier 2 also falling by a similar proportion. Deposits received also fell materially as these, along with a significant amount of lending, were part of the businesses sold. The Acceptances business remained, but the guarantees / performance bonds / self-liquidating contingencies businesses were sold.

THE INCOME STATEMENT OF A BANK

Given that the main business undertaken by banks is to lend to customers, using funds from deposits received and the inter-bank market, the primary source of income is net interest income, less loan loss expense. Also, given that interest margins can be very low, particularly for better-rated borrowers, most banks aim to enhance revenues with fee and commission incomes from derivatives, trade finance, investment banking, investment management, and other financial services operations. Some have proprietary trading desks, which aim to make profit through buying and selling of securities for the bank's own account, which entails the risk of loss, hence the added importance of assessing internal controls in this respect.

INCOME STATEMENT	31/12/X1 USD K	31/12/X2 USD K	31/12/X3 USD K	
Net Interest Income	13,357,425	8,623,390	7,544,927	63.2%
Loan Loss Expense & Provisions	-1,763,891	-1,087,435	-788,682	-6.6%
NET LENDING REVENUE	11,593,534	7,535,955	6,756,245	56.6%
Fee & Other Income	10,630,598	8,095,047	5,188,554	43.4%
NET REVENUE	22,224,132	15,631,002	11,944,799	100.0%
Personnel Costs	-3,193,197	-2,395,564	-1,776,361	-14.9%
Non-Loan Provision Charges Other Operating Expenses	-9,005,999	-6,707,901	-5,335,182	-44.7%
OPERATING EXPENSES	-12,199,196	-9,103,465	-7,111,543	-59.5%
PROFIT (LOSS) BEFORE TAX	10,024,936	6,527,537	4,833,256	40.5%
Tax Expense	-2,119,430	-1,673,447	-973,168	-8.1%
PROFIT (LOSS) AFTER TAX	7,905,506	4,854,090	3,860,088	32.3%
Proposed Dividend	-5,700,000	-3,700,000	-2,100,000	-17.6%
RETAINED PROFIT FOR YEAR	2,205,506	1,154,090	1,760,088	14.7%

XYZ's FX business was sold off, and reductions were seen in fee income elsewhere as previous major customers took some of their business to other banks. Operating costs reduced, the overall result being a significant fall in pre- and post- tax profit. After dividends and capital reserve movements, the revenue reserve was relatively stable.

CASH FLOW STATEMENT

The fair value of a share can be calculated by discounting forecast operational cash flow several years into the future, but most brokers tend to use the Income Statement as a useful proxy for this purpose. Apart from this, there is little value in assessing the cash flow statement for a bank, the reason being that financial institutions (unlike Corporates) do not have a predictable asset conversion cycle, cash flows being largely a function of sales and purchases of assets. The quality and liquidity of assets is therefore far more important, showing how quickly and easily assets can be converted into cash to meet obligations as they fall due. In addition, the availability of undrawn committed borrowing lines adds to the financial institution's liquidity profile.

RATIOS & OTHER CREDIT METRICS

An explanation of some useful measures is given below. In general, as an Analyst, you are looking for trends in the measures over at least a three-year period, though for annual reviews, a simple comparison of latest figures to previous year's is usually sufficient.

PROFITABILITY RATIOS

PROFITABILITY RATIOS	31/12/X1	31/12/X2	31/12/X3
Return on Assets	2.7%	3.0%	3.4%
Return on Risk Weighted Assets	4.2%	3.5%	4.1%
Return on Equity	21.9%	16.2%	31.9%
Effective Tax Rate	21.1%	25.6%	20.1%

Return On Assets, Return on Risk-Weighted Assets & Return on Equity

These can be calculated on a single year basis, or average of last two years, in terms of the ratio denominator. Also, the numerator can be either pre- or post -tax profit, but consistency is required across the years. In terms of the second ratio, the "Risk-Weighted Assets" figure is obtained from the published financial statements.

So, using pre-tax profit as numerator, and latest FYE figure for the denominator, the calculations are as follows:

Return on Assets = Profit Before Tax / Total Assets x 100 (%)

Return on RWA = Profit Before Tax / RW Assets x 100 (%)

Return on Equity = Profit Before Tax / Total Capital x 100 (%)

These show the overall profitability of the bank across the three denominator measures, again the analytical importance being a stable or upward trend, with any significant downtrends or negative ratios (representing losses) being commented upon. For XYZ Bank, measures have generally improved over the 3-year period as less profitable businesses have been sold.

Effective Tax Rate

This is calculated as Tax Expense / Profit Before Tax x 100 (%), showing the impact of tax on bottom-line profits. No major change has occurred for XYZ Bank over the 3-year period.

Other Profitability Ratios

Other ratios which can be calculated, information permitting, are:

Net Interest Margin

This is calculated as: (Gross Interest Income - Interest Expense) / Gross Interest Income x 100 (%), showing the fundamental profitability of the bank's lending business, and whether this has improved or declined over the period being analyzed.

Loan Loss Expense / Gross Interest Income (%)

This shows the extent to which revenue from lending has been depleted by losses on that lending. It should be borne in mind that banks need to make correct lending decisions in the vast majority of cases in order to be successful, a single big loss potentially wiping-out a significant portion of annual interest revenues.

REVENUE SPLIT

The Income Statement of your spreadsheet can be structured to contain a percentage split of component categories to Total Revenue, this showing the importance of each item. This can also be done for each year to show composition changes. Some of the more useful ratios are:

Operating Expenses / Net Revenue (%)

This shows the fundamental cost-base of all of the bank's operations, and you would expect to see a fairly stable position, or improvement, over the medium term, the reasons for any material deterioration being identified and commented upon within your analysis. .

Net Lending Revenue / Net Revenue

This shows the extent to which Net Lending Revenue (i.e. net interest income less loan losses) contribute to the bank's Net Revenue.

PERSONNEL STATISTICS

PERSONNEL STATISTICS	31/12/X1	31/12/X2	31/12/X3
Average Number of Employees	1,262,000	990,000	726,000
Cost Per Employee	2,530	2,420	2,447
Net Revenue Per Employee	17,610	15,789	16,453
Employee Costs / Net Revenue	14.4%	15.3%	14.9%
Employee Costs / Operating Expenses	26.2%	26.3%	25.0%

Cost Per Employee

This is calculated as Personnel Costs / Average Number of Employees. With the sale of businesses, XYZ Bank's employee number has naturally reduced, leaving the figures similar across the 3-year timeframe.

Net Revenue Per Employee

Calculated as Net Revenue / Average Number of Employees, this has moderately reduced for XYZ Bank over the 3-year period, but some recovery was seen in 20X3 compared to the previous year.

Employee Costs / Net Revenue

This ratio shows the relationship between one of the bank's main operating expenses, the cost of employing staff, and its primary sources of income, generally the lower the figure, the better. For XYZ Bank, the ratio has remained largely the same notwithstanding the business sales.

Employee Costs / Operating Expenses

This shows the impact which employee costs have on total operating costs within the bank. In the case of XYZ Bank, the situation has been pretty stable over the 3-year period.

LIQUIDITY RATIOS

These are essential for analyzing a financial institution's ability to meet its financial obligations as they fall due, in particular, calls by depositors for repayment.

LIQUIDITY & FUNDING RATIOS	31/12/X1	31/12/X2	31/12/X3
Loans Made / Total Funding	37.0%	55.7%	45.0%
Inter-Bank Borrowing / Loans Made	0.1%	1.4%	2.1%
Adj. Liquid Assets / Deposits Rec.	72.9%	65.2%	57.9%
Liquid Assets + Dep / Tot. Funding	65.5%	33.1%	31.4%
Demand Deposits / Total Funding	43.0%	50.6%	55.7%
Savings Deposits / Total Funding	2.9%	2.7%	1.7%
Time Deposits / Total Funding	43.8%	32.9%	24.8%
Inter-Bank Bor. / Total Funding	0.0%	0.8%	0.9%
Oth. Borrowings / Total Funding	10.2%	13.0%	16.9%

Loans Made / Total Funding

This ratio tells you how deposit monies received and borrowings have been on-lent to borrowing customers, The ratio rose for XYZ Bank, mainly as a result some larger deposit customers moving their monies to other, wider-scale, institutions.

Inter-Bank Borrowing / Loans Made

Some banks rely on inter-bank borrowings in order to fund their lending, the danger with this being that these borrowings tend to be shorter-term in practice than retail deposits (i.e. from personal customers). This makes the asset-liability maturity mismatch problem more of an issue if lending banks are unwilling to roll over their lending, creating a potential insolvency situation. This is exactly what happened to a bank in the UK, a former building society, which scaled-up its loan portfolio with monies borrowed from other financial institutions: When these lenders saw problems with the bank's financial position, they refused to continue with their loans when they matured, leading to collapse - That bank no longer exists, leading to shareholders losing their investments.

For XYZ Bank, the amount it borrows in the inter-bank market is very low, not representing a potential problem.

Adjusted Liquid Assets / Deposits Received

This is calculated as (Liquid Assets + Deposits Made - Interbank Borrowings) / Total Deposits Received, showing the ability of the bank to repay its depositors from available liquid assets. XYZ Bank's ratios have a deteriorating trend, deposits being covered by 57.9% as at 20X3. However, this coverage is acceptable in the context of the likely stability of the deposits, irrespective of their legal shorter-term maturities.

Liquid Assets + Deposits / Total Funding

This is calculated as (Liquid Assets + Deposits Made) / Total Funding, showing the bank's ability to meet all potential funding repayments from liquid assets. Again, for XYZ Bank there is a deteriorating trend, very similar to the situation above, and since most funding liabilities are retail deposits, the situation is acceptable.

Demand Deposits / Total Funding
Savings Deposits / Total Funding
Time Deposits / Total Funding
Interbank Borrowings / Total Funding
Other Borrowings / Total Funding

These ratios show the split of the bank's funding sources, and hence relative importance. Strictly speaking, the longer the legal maturity of the funding sources, the better, but most tend to be short-term, hence the usual asset-liability maturity mismatch for banks. For XYZ Bank, there is an increasing trend in demand deposits, whereby customers can obtain repayment immediately by asking the bank during normal working hours, and a reduction in time deposits (where a specified notice period is required), suggesting that customers wish to keep their holdings with the bank very liquid. This may be the result of customers looking for better opportunities elsewhere, which would be a concern if this leads to significant withdrawals in due course.

MATURITY PROFILES

As mentioned previously, a feature of the banking industry is an asset-liability maturity mismatch between legal maturity dates of loans and those of customer deposits, the former always on average being much longer than the latter, creating the potential for a liquidity crisis if depositors ask for their money back on mass. The fundamental problem is that a bank cannot obtain its lent funds back from borrowers until the legal maturity date and, if these are well into the future, there will be a long wait, so they are not generally available to meet depositors' repayment requirements. In practice, the potential for a liquidity crisis only occurs if a bank is approaching insolvency, or there are rumours of a bank's impending failure! I myself have experienced such a situation while working in Hong Kong several years' ago, when unfounded rumours led to depositors queuing round the block to get their money out. A week later, when the rumours were acknowledged as untrue, they re-deposited their money. In many developed markets, personal depositors are protected up to a certain limit by the State.

In the case of XYZ Bank, we can see the asset-liability mismatch very clearly, but as long as there is no financial crisis, the situation should be fine, the bank being required under banking regulations to hold sufficient liquid assets to cover likely customer withdrawals and other cash outgoings.

MATURITY PROFILE OF LOANS GIVEN	31/12/X1	31/12/X2	31/12/X3	
< 30 days	14,636,525	33,303,205	24,838,049	54.9%
30 days to 90 days	9,466,285	8,867,547	4,065,524	9.0%
90 days to 180 days	14,145,678	3,001,452	1,345,320	3.0%
180 days to 360 days	30,713,389	9,071,926	2,703,713	6.0%
> 360 days	22,457,192	12,935,974	12,250,799	27.1%
TOTAL LOANS GIVEN	91,419,069	67,180,104	45,203,405	100.0%
Re Balance Sheet	91,419,069	67,180,104	45,203,405	
MATURITY PROFILE OF CORE FUNDING				
< 30 days	202,566,271	88,997,975	58,911,926	70.6%
30 days to 90 days	10,188,465	5,455,070	14,961,973	17.9%
90 days to 180 days	9,344,545	10,055,889	9,243,500	11.1%
180 days to 360 days	25,199	428,621	335,778	0.4%
> 360 days				
TOTAL CORE FUNDING	222,124,480	104,937,555	83,453,177	100.0%
Re Balance Sheet	222,124,480	104,937,555	83,453,177	

ASSET QUALITY

Fundamental to a lending institution's success is its ability to lend to good quality customers who pay their borrowings back in accordance with agreed terms. In practice, for a bank to be successful, it needs to achieve near-100% accuracy in this respect for unsecured / uncollateralized lending, or be well-covered by securing assets or credit insurance for weaker customers, particularly those operating in difficult industry or geographical environments. Banks are usually strong enough to absorb a moderate level of bad debts, but not prolonged, large ones. The problem which banks face is the demands from shareholders and senior employees for profits (which impact dividends and bonuses), which could potentially lead to bad decisions being made. Counter to this is the need to be successful, not only in avoiding bad debts, but also not missing out on profitable opportunities - Being overly conservative in credit and other decisions can be almost as damaging as making bad decisions, so immense skill and judgement is required, not only technically, but also commercially.

ASSET QUALITY RATIOS	31/12/X1	31/12/X2	31/12/X3	
Performing Loans	87,997,502	65,135,429	43,768,722	96.8%
Non-Performing Loans	3,421,567	2,044,675	1,434,683	3.2%
Split as:				
Sub-Standard loans	1,368,627	817,870	573,873	1.3%
Doubtful Loans	1,197,548	715,636	502,139	1.1%
Bad Debts	855,392	511,169	358,671	0.8%
TOTAL LOANS	91,419,069	67,180,104	45,203,405	100.0%
Non-Performing Loans / Total Loans - Gross	3.7%	3.0%	3.2%	
Loan Loss Provision / Total Loans - Gross	3.8%	3.2%	3.4%	
Loan Loss Provision / Non-Performing Loans	101.7%	104.9%	106.1%	

Non-Performing Loans / Total Loans-Gross

This shows the ability of the bank to make good credit decisions, non-performing loans being defined as those which are bad debts and potential bad debts. The three categories are: "sub-standard" (the customer may be in financial difficulties, and a provision is being considered), "doubtful" (our lending is probably at risk, so a provision for some loss is made, taking into account collateral value, but there is some possibility of repayment being achieved) and "bad" (losses have been made and fully provisioned).

For XYZ Bank, the ratio is within acceptable norms, so we can conclude that there is no fundamental problem in its credit assessments. If the ratios were 5% or more, there could be a problem. From my experience, ratios can be very high in some emerging market banks, where credit assessment and staff quality is weaker on average than in major financial centres, so our exposure to such institutions will usually be on a collateralized basis for significant risks.

Loan Loss Provision / Total Loans-Gross

This is a similar ratio to the one above, but shows actual provisions made for bad and doubtful debts relative to loans granted. To clarify, a loan loss provision (a.k.a. reserve), is an accounting measure to recognise potential credit losses, these being deducted from gross loans given on the assets side of the balance sheet, also negatively impacting the bank's capital base. If recovery is made on loans for which provisions have been made, a positive adjustment is made.

Loan Loss Provisions / Non-Performing Loans

This shows the extent to which potential bad debts have been acknowledged in the bank's balance sheet, the "ideal" situation from a credit analytical perspective being full provisioning, so a ratio of 100%, or close to it.

For XYZ Bank, it seems to be moderately over-provisioning in 20X3, having greater provisions than potential losses, possibly owing to recoveries or reclassification of former non-performing loans as "performing", with provision adjustments still to be made. One would expect this ratio to come down to nearer 100% over time.

CAPITAL ADEQUACY

These measures are very much influenced by the Basel regulations, banks being required to maintain a sufficiently strong capital base, amongst other criteria.

	31/12/X1	31/12/X2	31/12/X3
CAPITAL ADEQUACY RATIOS			
Tier 1 Capital	36,445,542	33,468,036	11,617,978
Tier 2 Capital	9,237,585	6,909,788	3,525,804
Total Capital	45,683,127	40,377,824	15,143,782
Risk-Weighted Assets	240,190,380	188,843,452	118,715,386
Risk-Weighted Assets / Total Assets & Contingents	65.4%	88.2%	82.4%
Total Capital / Risk Weighted Assets	19.0%	21.4%	12.8%
Tier 1 Capital / Risk Weighted Assets	15.2%	17.7%	9.8%
Tier 1 Capital / Total Capital	79.8%	82.9%	76.7%
Total Capital / Net Loans Given	51.9%	62.1%	34.7%

Risk-Weighted Assets / Total Assets & Contingents

This ratio shows how the reported regulatory assessment of assets compares to the bank's balance sheet assets plus an add-on for assets related to contingent liabilities, figures below 100% showing how the assets have been weighted downwards by regulatory requirements.

For XYZ Bank, the ratio increased significantly in 20X2 owing to sale of lower-risk businesses (with lower expected revenue).

Total Capital / Risk-Weighted Assets
Tier 1 Capital / Risk-Weighted Assets

These show that there was a significant weakening in XYZ Bank's capital adequacy in 20X3, but remained well above regulatory requirements. This weakening largely arose owing to depletion of the bank's capital base through sale of businesses, combined with remaining businesses being more risky on average.

Tier 1 Capital / Total Capital

This shows the importance of Tier 1 capital to the bank's capital base, this being stable and proportionately high for XYZ Bank over the 3-year period.

Total Capital / Net Loans Given

This ratio shows the strength of the bank's capital base relative to the loan business it is writing, the higher the ratio the better from a financial analytical perspective. For XYZ Bank, a clear weakening is evident, something which needs to be closely watched when further accounts are published.

PROJECTIONS

Using information in the public domain (e.g. brokers' reports), Analysts should be able to construct formal projections showing the bank's expected financial condition over the next few years, this normally being done for a period covering the tenor of proposed limits. For XYZ Bank, consensus opinion is that it will remain stable, both in terms of revenues and balance sheet, over the next three years.

PEER GROUP ANALYSIS

It is usual to compare the specific financial institution you are analyzing to its main competitors, this allowing you to see its relative strengths and weaknesses by ratings and across a number of financial measures as covered in this chapter. Indeed, when organisations undertake their annual review of financial institutions to which they are exposed, it is quite common for this to be done on a bulk basis, using external ratings reports and tabulated financial criteria across all the banks being assessed, making it easy to see how exposures are spread across banks of differing strength. This portfolio view may therefore prompt assessment of whether exposure to a particular customer / counterparty is excessive by amount or tenor, enabling limit amendments.

CONCLUSION REGARDING XYZ BANK'S FINANCIAL WELL-BEING

The request for a short-term USD 50 million deposit with XYZ Bank looks reasonable in the context of the bank's size, having total capital and balance sheet assets of USD 15.1 billion and USD 119.7 billion respectively as at 31/12/X3. XYZ Bank's overall size has materially reduced owing to the business sales, but it remains a reasonably-sized player in its local market. Its external ratings have consequently fallen to bottom-end investment rating level, but given the short-term nature of the proposed exposure, we can decide whether to reduce or fully withdraw if there is further material deterioration, the likelihood of this being minimal based on information in the public domain. The bank's internal controls in terms of operating risk, market risk and credit risk, are all satisfactory and in line with banking best practice.

Chapter 5
ANALYZING NON-BANK FINANCIAL INSTITUTIONS

NON-BANK LENDING INSTITUTIONS

These can be analyzed in much the same way as banks, their product offerings being simpler, and often focused on relatively small personal loans or fully-secured mortgage lending. Main additional issues to consider are extent of external regulation to ensure that the lender remains financially-sound; potentially unsavoury activities, such as charging extortionately high interest rates, which (though legal) may be morally inappropriate, and concentration risks (such as closely-correlated lending leading to significant losses if certain events, local deterioration, etc. occur.

If significant weaknesses are identified, it may be inappropriate to be exposed to these entities, at least not on an unsecured / uncollateralised basis. Of course, in taking security / collateral, you would need to ensure that it can be sold at a reasonable price if the institution runs into difficulties and defaults. As a Credit Officer, I have personally seen cases where security offered has consisted of buildings situated in very undesirable locations; property of a very specialized nature, which cannot be converted for other uses; aged pipes and tanks, which have no realizable value after extraction; old computer equipment, which has been super-ceded by much better devices, and shares in near-worthless private companies, amongst others. At the end of the day, if you are going to take security, it needs to have a meaningful realizable value in the context of your exposure, and you must have an unassailable right to sell it in need. However, my advice is generally not to rely on security as a reason for lending, but make sure that the case is good on its own merits, taking security as a back-up measure should things not go to plan. Also, factor the moral implications into your lending decision, as well as potential negative reputation to your organisation of the proposed lending and of realising security.

BROKER-DEALERS / SECURITIES FIRMS

These are organizations which engage in the business of trading securities and other financial instruments for their own account ("dealer" or "trader") or on behalf of customers ("broker"). Many broker-dealers are business units or subsidiaries of banks and investment companies. Such businesses are regulated by the Securities and Exchange Commission (SEC) in the United States; the Financial Conduct Authority (FCA) in the United Kingdom; the Financial Services Agency in Japan, or local regulatory authorities in other countries.

In analyzing such firms, it is again important to understand how regulations impact financial statements and operations, internal controls being very important. Particularly for dealers, who trade for the organisation's own account, there is great potential for significant losses through ineffective market risk controls, and unauthorised activities by so-called "rogue traders" through weak operational risk controls. Whilst huge profits can be made through dealing, firms which offer pure broking and matched-principal trading are the safest from a credit risk perspective, their continued existence being based on their ability to get and maintain fee / commission income. Successful companies' strategic strength is therefore to transact efficiently and without error, operating risks being well controlled, with little potential for market risk losses. Agency / broking operations arise where the firm acts purely as an intermediary between buyer and seller. Matched-principal trading is similar, except that the firm takes a position in the security, but this is covered by a counter-position with a third party. In both cases, there is potential counterparty risk if the party selling the security fails to deliver owing to insolvency, in which case the broker will need to purchase it in the market at prevailing market price to deliver it to the buyer. Similarly, if a buyer becomes insolvent before taking delivery of, and paying for, a security sold by a third party to the broker, the broker will theoretically need to sell it into the Market, so takes the risk that price moves adversely between purchase and sale. In such situations, the broker will attempt to recover these costs from the defaulting third party, but if that party is insolvent, this may be problematical.

INSURANCE COMPANIES

Analyzing insurance companies can be quite difficult for the "layman", particularly given the industry-specific terminology used in financial statements and third-party reports. However, essentially the same macro- and micro- environmental issues apply to insurance companies as for any financial institution, as do internal controls covering operating risk, market risk and credit risk, as covered later in this book. To provide guidance to those interested, I have written a separate book on how to analyze insurance companies of all types, entitled, "Insurance Company Financial & Risk Analysis" which covers this specialized topic.

FUNDS MANAGEMENT FIRMS & FUNDS

Fund (or Asset) Management firms offer collective investment schemes, such as mutual funds, exchange-traded funds (e.g. UK investment trusts) and hedge funds, also offering dealing services. As with other types of financial institution, activities include employing professional staff; researching individual assets and asset classes; settlement; marketing; internal auditing, and producing reports for clients. Apart from marketers and fund managers, there are Compliance staff (to ensure that the firm acts in accordance with legislative and regulatory requirements); internal auditors (to ensure adequacy of, and adherence to, internal systems and controls); financial controllers (to manage the firm's own money and costs); IT staff, and "back office" employees, who track and record transactions and fund valuations for clients.

In transacting with a fund management firm, it is usually the case that the latter acts as Agent on behalf of an underlying fund or funds as Principal(s). For large transactions, it is therefore appropriate to analyze the underlying fund(s) in detail, these being your main source of repayment, as well as the capabilities of the fund management firm acting on its behalf. Sometimes, the fund management firm transacts on behalf of a huge number of underlying funds for relatively low-risk transactions (e.g. securities trading or short-term FX trading), making it impractical to analyze every underlying fund, so a simple limit is set at fund management firm level as Agent.

Understanding legal recourse as above is essential, but one also needs to take into account the nature of the fund management firm and location of the underlying funds which it manages. Mutual funds, unit trusts and pension funds are generally relatively "lower-risk" entities in that there is a strict limit on permitted borrowing and the nature of investments. However, hedge funds tend to be effectively unregulated (except in certain jurisdictions, such as Delaware in the USA); often based offshore (e.g. in the British Virgin Islands; Bermuda; Netherlands Antilles, etc.), and capable of investing in practically anything. In all cases, it is essential to understand the intended investments of the fund; extent of potential leverage, and the capabilities of the fund management firm, including experience of staff and internal controls. Analysis of the funds' and fund management firm's prospectuses and financial statements can be very useful here. One thing which will strike you immediately is the high fees charged by some hedge fund managers as performance fees, sometimes 20% or more of profits generated in a given period. The size of funds / assets under management, and how this has changed over the past few years, is usually a good indicator as to the quality of the fund management firm: Successful firms will have a high and increasing level, whereas less successful ones will have a significantly reducing one as customers extract their monies for investment elsewhere.

In analyzing a particular fund, an Analyst will look at the composition and quality of assets (being mainly securities held as investments), quality being a factor of liquidity and price volatility. Investments which can be sold quickly and easily on a stock exchange, without significant loss, can be considered high quality. However, certain assets are more volatile than others, the price of equities moving much more widely on a day-to-day basis than quoted bonds, for example. On the liabilities side of the balance sheet, the Analyst will look at the amount borrowed by the fund to finance its investment purchases, this being called leverage, as well as any cap on this leverage. The higher the leverage, the more risky the fund. The Analyst will also look at the fund's capital base, namely its Net Asset Value ("NAV") to see how it has changed from period to period, a well-managed fund generally increasing in value from year to year through good performance and, if it is open-ended, additional investments. The investment strategy of the fund must be understood, and this should be clearly stated, the Analyst assessing any potential weaknesses and concentrations.

Mutual / pension fund limits, and those for fund managers for lower-risk business, are often set on a matrix-style basis, a table being produced covering the funds for which limits are sought, together with basic details covering activity of the fund; total assets; NAV;

return / profit details, and any performance ratings (e.g. by Morningstar), etc. For equities and debt trading, limits are often set at the fund manager level owing to the fact that single transactions often cover a number of funds, and it is administratively difficult to set individual limits for a large number of funds.

Chapter 6
ASSESSING OPERATIONAL RISK INTERNAL CONTROLS

Operational risk relates to risk of loss through poor management and control (e.g. the activities of rogue traders); failure to execute documentation correctly or make margin calls, and any other form of human, technological or process error. It can also include other classes of risk, such as fraud, security, privacy protection, legal risks, physical (e.g. infrastructure shutdown) or environmental risks. In effect, operational risk is reduced through good management and practices within the firm, failure potentially leading to direct financial losses, as well as indirect losses through depletion of client satisfaction and the firm's reputation.

Unlike credit risks, market risks and insurance risks, operational risks cannot be diversified away, meaning that, as long as people, systems and processes remain imperfect, operational risk cannot be fully eliminated. Whilst perfection may not be achievable, risk reduction can be achieved subject to balancing the costs of improvement against the expected benefits.

Until Basel II reforms to banking supervision, operational risk was viewed as a residual category reserved for risks and uncertainties which were difficult to quantify and manage in traditional ways, being a function of good regulatory and corporate governance. Events such as the World Trade Centre disaster; rogue trading at various banks, and losses incurred daily through organized crime's fraudulent activities, highlight the fact that good risk management goes beyond market risk and credit risk issues.

The identification and measurement of operational risk is an important topic for banks, particularly given the Basel Committee's requirement, under Basel II, to implement a capital charge for this risk in determining capital adequacy. Basel II regards the following items as operational risk: (i) Internal Fraud: Misappropriation of assets, tax evasion, intentional mis-marking of positions and bribery. (ii) External Fraud: Theft of information, hacking damage, third-party theft and forgery. (iii) Employment Practices and Workplace Safety: Discrimination, workers compensation, employee health and safety. (iv) Clients, Products, and Business Practice: Market manipulation, anti-trust activities, improper trade, product defects, fiduciary breaches, account churning. (v) Damage to Physical Assets: Natural disasters, terrorism and vandalism. (vi) Business Disruption and Systems Failures: Utility disruptions, software and hardware failures. (vii) Execution, Delivery, and Process Management: Data entry errors, accounting errors, failed mandatory reporting, and negligent loss of client assets.

The problem is that it is relatively difficult to identify or assess levels of operational risk and its many sources. However, many organisations now collect data on operational losses, using this data to model operational risk and calculate a capital reserve against future operational losses. In addition to the Basel II requirement for banks, this is now a requirement for European insurance firms under Solvency II, the insurance industry's equivalent legislation for capital adequacy.

There are three approaches for measuring operational risk under the Basel regulations: (i) Basic Indicator Approach, based on annual revenue of the Financial Institution. (ii) Standardized Approach, based on annual revenue of each of the broad business lines of the Financial Institution, (ii) Advanced Measurement Approaches, based on the internally developed risk measurement framework of more sophisticated banks.

Chapter 7
ASSESSING MARKET RISK INTERNAL CONTROLS

OVERVIEW

Market risk refers to the risk of adverse movement in the value of assets, for example interest rates, foreign currency exchange rates, market price of equities or market price of commodities, resulting in a loss to the organisation. Therefore, when a financial institution enters into various transactions, it will set limits as to the amount of risk it is willing to take overall, for example using a measure called "Value at Risk" ("VaR"), as well as limits for individual products and assets. Beyond these limits, it will hedge its risk, usually on a bulk basis.

Some banks adopt the policy of fully hedging interest rate risk in their Banking Book business through transfer to the Trading Book, this then either being hedged by the bank's financial markets unit, or marked against agreed limits. Various methods are used to determine whether the bank's estimation of market risk is sufficiently accurate and conservative, including stress testing and scenario testing.

Market Risk is generally managed through the financial institution's Trading Book, the Banking Book being used to record non-market risk activities. Whilst the bank's Board of Directors has ultimate responsibility for the management of market risk, it will delegate responsibility for reviewing exposures; hedging strategy; risk management processes; approval of market risk limits; instruments to be traded; measurement assumptions, and asset valuation methodology to a separate committee, often called the Treasury Asset & Liability Committee ("TALCO"), or something similar. In turn, this Committee delegates some of these day-to-day responsibilities to the Head of Risk Management and his / her Market Risk unit. The bank's Audit & Internal Control department and Committee independently ensures that risks are well measured, monitored and managed.

There are various ways of estimating market risk for individual product types, this being directly related to the estimation of replacement cost in determining counterparty risk in trading and derivatives transactions. The most favoured method (in accuracy terms) used by more sophisticated banks is to calculate maximum Potential Future Exposure("PFE") using Monte Carlo simulation.

TYPES OF MARKET RISK

The key specific types of market risk experienced by a financial institution are: (i) Interest rate risk: the potential change in interest rates which lead to change in value of assets, for example quoted bonds - These tend to increase in value with expectation of a reduction in interest rates, and vice versa. Structural interest rate risk arises from financial flows and assets / liabilities rather than from trading activities. (ii) Equity risk, being the change in market price of equities; i.e. quoted shares. (iii)

FX risk, being change in currency exchange rates. (iv) Commodity risk - The change in commodity prices.

Market risk arises through (i) "Trading Book" activities as above, the price of financial instruments potentially also being influenced by spread risk, basis risk, correlation-specific and volatility risk. (ii) "Banking Book" activities, this either being fully hedged or transferred to the Trading Book.

MANAGEMENT OF MARKET RISK

This is largely achieved by setting limits, and monitoring / reporting exposures. Limits are usually set in a hierarchy, with an overall Market Risk limit; a second level for separate bank legal entities and branches; a third level for trading desks, and a fourth level for each product type.

MARKET RISK CATEGORIES

In essence, Market Risk is composed of the following three categories of risk: (i) Price Risk: This is where value potentially changes as a result of changes in underlying "Market Risk Factors", where the Trading Book has non-zero "Market Risk Factor Sensitivities". A "Market Risk Factor" is any price, rate, volatility, correlation or other factor (traded or non-traded) which is used to value a financial instrument. A "Market Risk Factor Sensitivity" is defined as the change in the base currency value of the Trading Book arising from a one unit change in a Market Risk Factor, other things being equal. (ii) Basis Risk: This is a portfolio risk that arises when positions exist which are generally offsetting, but are subject to different Market Risk Factors. The nature of the risk is to movements in Market Risk Factors of financial instruments, that are not correlated (or not sufficiently correlated), leading to a change in the base currency value of a position. In other words, basis risk is the financial risk that offsetting investments in a hedging strategy will not experience price changes in entirely opposite directions from each other. This imperfect correlation between the two investments creates the potential for excess gains or losses in a hedging strategy, thus adding risk to the position. (iii) Market Liquidity Risk: This is defined as the risk of loss that may arise as a result of an inability to liquidate a position due to the illiquidity of a market. The magnitude of this risk is a function of the products and markets the bank trades, and the size of positions that it may hold relative to the market.

RISK MEASUREMENTS

Some risk measurements have a limit applied to them, others being used for monitoring purposes via a reporting mechanism. The most common measures used by a bank are (i) Marking to market ("MtM"). (ii) Value at Risk ("VaR"), set at 1 day and 10-day holding periods, based on 95% and 99% confidence levels for each. (iii) Value stress testing, which consists of shifting risk factors and comparing the resulting MtM against the base MtM. (iv) Scenario testing, being the application of specific scenarios (such as the WTC disaster or Asian crisis) to the current portfolio, to derive valuations for comparison with results from current market data. (v) Stop losses. Cumulative Loss Limits ensure that, in the event of continued losses from a trading activity, the trading activity is stopped and the circumstances leading to the losses are reviewed by senior management before trading is resumed. (vi) Position limits, which control the amount of an instrument held (short or long positions), and therefore control exposure to movements in price. (vii) Back-testing, used to validate the VaR model. (viii) Supplementary limits, used to enable Risk Management to control the nature and scale of certain higher-risk trading activities, examples being a limit on the number of deals per day by product group and desk, and a limit on single transaction size at product group level.

VALUE AT RISK ("VaR")

Definition

VaR is a statistical approach which quantifies risk using the actual or assumed distribution of potential changes to the value of a portfolio (profit or loss) as a result of changes in Market Risk Factors, being any price, rate, volatility, correlation or other factor (traded or non-traded) which is used to value a financial instrument, examples being interest rates, FX rates, commodity prices and equity prices. Different confidence levels can be used in the probability distribution analysis, but common approaches are VaR calculated at 95% and 99% confidence levels over a one and ten day holding period. What VaR effectively tells senior management is that, at the confidence level used, the bank has USD x million of market risk exposure during the relevant period. As a side issue, a similar measure can be used to quantify Credit Risk for a bank, this being called Credit VaR.

Monte Carlo Simulation

A "Monte Carlo simulation" approach is often used to calculate VaR, this involving modelling of potential value changes for a defined time horizon over a large number of possible scenarios. This results in thousands of simulations, each one reflecting a different potential outcome. When all of the simulations are run, they are listed in order of the biggest gain to the biggest loss, and a cut-off point is determined based on the selected confidence level. The loss at that cut-off point is the VaR amount.

Market Risk Factors

For FX risk, risk factors relate to individual foreign currencies, the risk arising from changes in values of these foreign currencies to domestic currency also being captured. Market liquidity, event and settlement date mismatch risks are covered in the simulations.

For interest rate risk, a bank will usually incorporate (i) re-pricing risk, differences arising between the timing of rate changes and cash flows; (ii) yield curve risk, arising from changing rate relationships across the range of maturities; (iii) basis risk, which arises from changing rate relationships among yield curves that affect the institution's activities, and (iv) option risks, arising from options embedded in certain products. Interest rate risk for each currency is usually calculated separately.

For equity risk, risk factors correspond to each of the equity markets in which the bank has positions. The measurement of equity risk captures exposure to price movements in the overall equity market index; specific sectors of the equity market, such as industry, cyclical and non-cyclical sectors, and individual equity issues where appropriate.

For commodity risk, in addition to changes in spot prices, commodities also incur basis risk (the risk that the relationship between prices of similar commodities alters though time); interest rate risk (the risk of a change in the cost of carry for forward positions and options) and forward gap risk (the risk that the forward price may change for reasons other than a change in interest rates). Commodities trading activities also account for variations in the "convenience yield" between derivatives positions, such as forwards and swaps, and cash positions in the commodity.

Back-Testing

This is the process whereby actual daily profits and losses are compared with calculated VaR exposures in order to assess the quality and accuracy of the VaR model. The one-day back-testing process, taken over a one day holding period, involves calculating a profit & loss figure for the one-day period by deducting current value yesterday from current value today, and comparing this with the previous day's VaR amount.

An accurate approach to testing the model is to use the portfolio as it was one day ago against today's rates in order to produce a current value. This means re-calculating the value of yesterday's portfolio using yesterday's date but today's market rates. A quicker and simpler, but less accurate approach, is to ignore the fact that the portfolio will have changed during the holding period, trades maturing overnight and new trades executed. Using this approach, it is assumed that, by and large, maturing trades will be reinvested, so the portfolio will not have changed significantly. With both approaches, an allowance is made for the fact that the VaR figure could reasonably be less than actual difference in value (in theory, for a 95% confidence level, there is a 5% chance of this happening) by reporting over a 250 day historical period. More than 10 violations during the last 250 days is generally considered to be the point at which the VaR model needs improvement.

Scenario & Stress Testing

Usually undertaken on at least a monthly basis, scenario testing checks the impact of both the current environment and the models used on the measured risk of the financial institution. The bank may choose scenarios based on either analyzing historical data or empirical models of changes in Market Risk Factors, Monte Carlo simulation generally being adopted in this respect. The objective will be to allow the bank to assess the effects of sizeable changes in Market Risk Factors on its holdings and financial condition. Scenarios chosen will include low-probability adverse scenarios that could result in extraordinary losses. Scenario analysis and stress tests will take into account the effects of unusual changes in market and non-Market Risk Factors, including prices, volatilities, market liquidity, historical correlations and assumptions in stressed market conditions. The size of shocks implicit in the stress tests should be sufficient to cover movements as large as could reasonably be expected within a 10- to 20- year period. Stress tests include: (i) Parallel and non-parallel yield curve shifts of arbitrary amounts. (ii) Sigma shifts of the short rate (with sympathetic yield curve shifts) by any number of standard deviations desired by the user. (iii) Probability shifts, to get the percentile ranking of portfolio valuations. (iv) Volatility shifts, to measure the impact of changes in interest rate volatility on value. (v) Mean reversion shifts, to measure the sensitivity of value to changes in the length and severity of interest rate cycles. A good way to stress test is to model a series of unusual events. Stress tests may model the impact of abnormal market conditions, or change in the measured amount of VaR that occurs when other simulation assumptions are at extreme levels.

EXCESS MANAGEMENT

Excesses over Market Risk limits can arise as a result of trading activity (usually new trades), and also owing to day-to-day movement in market prices, the bank's Market Risk unit monitoring and reporting the situation to senior management for suitable action, such as closing out positions, if considered necessary. The bank should have procedures in place for traders to check that new trades will not exceed limits before the trade is confirmed, with formal approval sought from Risk Management for any excess prior to confirmation of the deal. In the case of an unauthorised excess, there is likely to be disciplinary action through the Human Resources department, sometimes involving dismissal under a "three strikes and you're out" rule. In the case of pre-approved excesses, there will be a temporary limit increase to cover the agreed amount. In the case of market movements, the situation will generally be monitored by the Market Risk unit, with appropriate management reporting.

PROPRIETARY TRADING BOOK LIMITS

Proprietary trading book limits represent limits set on broad categories of securities purchased for the firm's own book. Thus, they are portfolio management limits to provide a measure of diversification within the trading portfolio. Subject to certain criteria, dealers can purchase securities provided these limits are not breached.

Securities Concentration

Limits are set by covering specific securities categories, common examples being: (i) Money Market Book; (ii) Bond Trading Book (iii) Emerging Markets Debt Trading Book, and (iv) Equity Book.

Issuer Concentration

Limits are set to ensure that no unacceptable concentrations of risk on the same issuing company / group build up across various "books" and "portfolios".

Other Limits

Each Portfolio or Book will usually have the following Limits and Sub-Limit classifications: (i) Maximum Overall Proprietary Book Limit; (ii) Income at Stake Limit for the Portfolio or Book; (iii) Maximum Percentage or USD Amount permitted per Issuer; (iv) Maximum Country Concentration Limits; (v) Maximum Holding Period of any Trade; (vi) Maximum Short Position (where short positions are permitted), and (vii) Maximum Other Instruments, such as options, swaps, etc. Others might be: (i) Maximum Amount of Debt (Bonds or Commercial Paper); (ii) Maximum non-Investment Rating Bonds/Debt; (iii) Maximum Equity (iv) Maximum Percentage or USD Amount permitted per Issue; (v) Maximum Local / Foreign Currency components; (vi) Maximum Government securities (T-Bills, T-Bonds); (vii) Maximum Private Sector securities (corporate bonds, equities); (viii) Minimum Average Daily Trading Volume (i.e. Liquidity) (over the last 12 months), and (ix) Maximum Industry Concentration.

Chapter 8
ASSESSING CREDIT RISK INTERNAL CONTROLS

THE BOARD OF DIRECTORS

Credit risk management within a firm is ultimately overseen by the Board of Directors (as are all activities), who delegate certain responsibilities to various committees, examples being an Executive Committee; and Audit & Internal Control Committee, and the Credit Committee(s). All policies and practices relating to credit risk within the bank are ultimately approved by the Board and relevant Committees.

DEFINITION OF CREDIT & COUNTERPARTY RISK

In essence, "credit risk" is the potential loss arising from lending to a third party and that third party failing to repay. In a similar vein, "counterparty risk" is the potential loss arising from contracting with a third party to buy or sell securities or derivatives, and the third party fails to fulfil its contractual obligations. Credit and counterparty risk are often simply called "credit risk" as an all-encompassing term.

TYPES OF CREDIT & COUNTERPARTY RISK

Credit risk usually arises through the transaction types described below. Of these, all but Pre-settlement Risk are 100 % risk-weighted in terms of calculating exposure level, being the full transaction amount, irrespective of whether there is any security / collateral. Pre-settlement risk, covering trading, derivatives, stock borrowing & lending and repos / reverse repos, is estimated based on the probability of market price movements, eligible collateral being deducted to derive limit utilization amount.

LENDING & CONTINGENT RISK

Lending is where money is given to a customer, but required to be repaid subject to agreed terms. Contingent risk is unfunded exposure, representing the potential risk of loss should the customer fail to perform certain specified actions or default. - Common examples are demands for payment under letters of credit or guarantees issued by the bank on behalf of its customers. Contingent limits tend to be of a committed nature, but (subject to facility wording) may be uncommitted for any unutilised portion of the limit.

Deposits Held With Third Party Financial Institutions

The financial institution will have deposits with various banks, so incurs credit risk on these banks.

Mortgages

These are loans provided to people and firms to purchase property, the property acting as security for the lending.

Personal Loans

These are loans to individuals for a set period, principal repayment (plus interest charge) usually being on an amortising basis, usually monthly.

Overdraft Facilities

Overdrafts are credit facilities where the customer is permitted to borrow on its current account by withdrawing more money than is in the account. Repayment is "on demand", meaning that the provider of the facility can seek repayment simply by asking, the borrower being legally obliged to repay immediately during working hours. These facilities are used by personal customers and firms to meet short-term liquidity requirements.

Short-term Revolving Credit Facilities

Short-term revolving credit facilities are a form of working capital funding, used by firms to cover timing differences in cash flows, the borrower being obliged to repay within an agreed set timeframe (e.g. 3 months, 6 months, 1 year), but borrowings often being immediately redrawn (a.k.a. "rolled over") assuming that the lender considers the borrower to remain a good credit risk.

Bilateral Loans

This is where a lender provides a loan to a firm for a specified period, with repayment being made on an amortizing basis (e.g. monthly, 3-monthly, 6-monthly or yearly); via a "bullet" repayment (principal repaid all in one go at the end), or with a repayment holiday (e.g. no principal repayment for a set period, and amortising thereafter), usually to align with expected cash flows.

Club Deals

Here, two or three banks join forces to provide a loan to a customer, one of the banks being the lead bank, handling administrative activities.

Syndicated Loans

This is where a number of banks provide a large loan to a customer, the latter normally being a major corporate or financial institution. One of the banks is Agent, acting as the contact point between the banking syndicate and the customer, and handling loan administrative duties, including managing provision of information, financial covenant compliance certificates, etc.

Trade Finance

These facilities relate to lending services provided to customers who are trading goods locally and internationally, these tending to be short-term, self-securing transactions for the bank. Examples are discounting of bills of exchange, whereby the bank purchases these at a price lower than their face value, presenting them for payment at maturity, the difference between discount price and face value being the interest charge. The bank may also accept bills and notes for a fee (a form of unfunded "financing"), effectively guaranteeing them, allowing the customer to sell them in the Market, and the bank making payment to the holder at maturity, recovering this from the customer's current account at that point. Documentary letters of credit (L/Cs) are where the bank acts on behalf of its importing customers in contractually agreeing to make payment to the exporter's bank upon presentation of agreed documents. A bank may also "confirm" L/Cs issued by other banks, guaranteeing their payment. A bank may also provide performance guarantees (a.k.a. performance bonds), whereby it agrees to make payment to a buyer if its customer fails to perform its contract, a form of contingent risk. Other similar forms of guarantee are those given to tax and customs authorities for payment of tax and duties, and those confirming repayment of advance payments under certain conditions.

Project Finance

For these, banks provide financing for specified large projects, such as building of a shopping complex or other large structure, the borrower usually being a standalone special purpose vehicle ("SPV") owned by the sponsors, but with recourse to the SPV only. In effect, the risk is on the viability of the project, the bank needing to ensure that generated cash flows will be sufficient to achieve repayment of the lending, interest and other costs. Also, security will be taken over the project assets, the value of these increasing as the construction progresses, often having limited value in the early stages. Also, cash flows will be controlled, often using escrow accounts, and a possible cash sweep to ensure that any excess cash generated is used for the bank's benefit.

Structured Finance

These are similar to project financings, but generally of a smaller size. An example is where a bank purchases a lease from another financier, the lessee usually being unaware of the sale. In such cases, the bank needs to ensure that the documentation gives rights over the leased asset, and cash flows are routed to the bank, held in escrow as appropriate.

Securitizations

Securitization units of banks will take a portfolio of lending assets; transfer these assets into a Special Purpose Vehicle ("SPV"), and sell shares / securities in the SPV to investors, retaining a small percentage (e.g. 5-

10%) as a sign of its confidence in the quality of the portfolio. The advantage for the bank is that it is effectively off-loading most of its credit risk in relation to the portfolio to the third-party investors, enabling it to then make more loans and securitize them in the future. An example of securitizations are collateralized debt obligations ("CDOs"), whereby the portfolio of debt assets is securitized as above, the ratings agencies assigning ratings to various tranches of security based on the likelihood of loss. The potential problem is that, if the underlying assets are weak (e.g. a portfolio of credit card doubtful debts, or mortgages over poor-quality houses in undesirable areas), the ratings assigned to the securities may not be as accurate as one would hope, leading to losses. During the banking crisis a few years' ago, many banks purchased large tranches of such debt, obtaining approval for this via their Asset-Liability Committees, but circumventing their Credit Risk departments. The result was that the investments made had much higher credit risk than anticipated, leading to material losses. In some cases, the holders of the investments were unable to enforce security / collateral over the underlying loans since there was no documentation rights for them to do this, these being held with the original lenders.

This is one reason why Basel regulations have been tightened up in recent years, but demonstrates how bad management and bad investment choices can bring otherwise solid banks to their proverbial knees. On the subject of bad investments, several years' ago, senior management of one of the biggest banks in the world decided that it needed to expand its activities geographically. It therefore purchased a bank in another country, which was known to have a very high concentration risk on a particular industry sector. Unfortunately, this industry sector ran into serious problems, leading to customers of that bank becoming insolvent, with significant losses resulting. The purchasing bank no longer exists, having been taken over by another bank to prevent collapse!

ISSUER RISK

This type of Credit risk relates to investments in quoted bonds (the term also applying to equities, but not in a Credit context) which are expected to be held for a fairly long length of time, so are regarded as credit risks rather than trading risks. A common cut-off period in this respect is 6 months, so any debt instrument expected at purchase to be held longer will be treated as credit risk.

UNDERWRITING RISK

This relates to underwriting of syndicated lending and issued debt securities, which means agreeing to take on the whole risk amount, with expected sell-down within a given period, say 18 months. Underwriting risk can be analyzed by a number of components, namely: (i) Issuer Risk. (ii) Pricing Risk. (iii) Market Risk. (iv) Event Risk. (v) Distribution Risk. (vi) Reputational Risk, if the distribution fails. Most banks treat the risk over and above hold level (i.e. participation in the syndicated ending or holding of debt) as market risk, though a credit risk process is usually followed in approving such exposures. In making the decision as to whether to accept underwriting risk, the syndications unit of the bank will need to make a strong case that sell-down / distribution of the debt can be achieved within the stated timeframe, this being determined through discussion with potential institutional buyers. "Best efforts" underwriting is where the bank does not accept legal responsibility for the full debt amount, so the overall debt level could be theoretically reduced by any amounts unsold / undistributed by the end of the distribution period.

COUNTERPARTY RISK

Definition

Counterparty / credit risk relates to any potential loss as a result of the failure of a party with which the bank has contracted. For direct lending to that party (e.g. money market lending and precious metal lending and leasing), it is the failure to repay. Repos and stock lending can be viewed as collateralized direct lending, the risk being the difference between the amount lent / borrowed and the current MtM (mark-to-market) value of the collateral, many banks recording this difference as Pre-Settlement risk, with an added Settlement limit where repayment is on a non-DVP ("delivery-v-payment") basis.

Product Types

This is usually split by Pre-settlement Risk, with additional Settlement Risk limits for non-DVP (Delivery-v-Payment) settlement / delivery. Common product types are forwards, options and swaps on FX, interest rates, commodities and equities. For options, counterparty PFE risk arises on options purchased, with only premium settlement risk incurred for options sold, where premium (i.e. the "fee" paid for the option) is deferred (i.e. not paid upfront).

Counterparty Types

The bank's Financial Markets unit / division will tend to transact with the following types of counterparty: "Corporates" (industrial, manufacturing, etc.); securities companies, brokers and commodities trading firms; banks; other lending institutions, such as building societies; insurance companies, and funds / fund managers.

Financial Markets Division Set-Up

Front Office Trading Activities

The fundamental "component" of a bank's Financial Markets division is the Trading Floor, which houses traders and salespersons, together with all hardware needed to do their jobs, the major ones being information screens, tools to enable calculations for trading strategies, and the Front Office Trading system. The latter is particularly important as it facilitates trades with customers; advises Traders of counterparty risk and market risk limits and availability, and should provide predeal checking to show any potential breach of limits before a trade is executed. Salespersons are responsible for obtaining business with clients and potential clients, and are often on the same desks / teams as traders, who execute transactions with clients and market counterparties. Desks are usually established by nature of product given the specialised skills of traders, for example: Fixed-Income (i.e. bonds trading); Equities; Commodities; Stock Borrowing & Lending; Repos; Forex and Credit derivatives.

Middle & Back Office Activities

Other units can also be located on the trading floor, including Settlements, Counterparty Risk, Market Risk, Compliance and Legal, the aim being to provide quick and easy interaction with Salespersons and Traders. The Settlements unit in a bank is responsible for ensuring that all securities trading and brokerage transactions are completed successfully, with any failed trades being investigated and reported to appropriate management, including Counterparty Risk Management. Related Middle Office functions, in conjunction with Counterparty Risk Systems staff, will ensure that trades are correctly allocated to limits and that any netting of transactions and collateral is handled correctly. The ability to net depends on the adequacy of legal documentation in place. In the absence of completed Netting and Collateral Agreements, Long-Form Confirmations will be used and, if correctly signed-off by the counterparty, may permit netting to occur (subject to Legal's verification and internal policy).

The Nostro Accounts unit is responsible for cash accounts with third party financial institutions, including monitoring of balances, referring any potential / actual excesses over internal limits (usually soft - i.e. used for monitoring only, rather than being advised to the customer) to Counterparty Risk Management and other senior management. The Custodian Account unit is responsible for custodian accounts with third party financial institutions, the latter often being the same banks with which nostro accounts are held. The Unit will monitor the value of securities and other assets (including precious metals) held with the custodian, advising Counterparty Risk Management of any potential / actual excesses over internal limits (again usually soft). The Collateral Management unit, which liaises with Custodian Account Monitoring & Control, controls and monitors liquid assets given to the bank by counterparties, ensuring that the type and value given is in accordance with legal documentation (i.e. Credit Support Documentation relating to a Master Agreement, or a standalone Collateral Agreement). The Unit will also make margin calls in accordance with such agreements. The Compliance department s responsible for ensuring that the bank's activities comply with all applicable regulations, including money laundering / KYC ("know your customer") checks, and handling of potential breaches of Large Exposure Capital Base rules. The Legal department is responsible for issuing and negotiating documentation with customers.

Pre-Settlement Risk

Pre-settlement Risk limits are used for trading activities, derivatives, collateralised stock borrowing & lending and repo / reverse repo transactions, representing the potential risk of loss should default occur prior to settlement. Utilisation of pre-settlement limits is based on an estimate of loss in the event of default (replacement cost), which will generally be much lower than the nominal value. Pre-settlement Limits are always uncommitted, only the utilisations being committed subject to agreed trade terms. For trading transactions, the risk of loss is the estimate of the expense involved in replacing the contract by a trade with another counterparty at the then prevailing (possibly unfavourable) market price. In other words, the (potential or expected) risk is the cost to the financial institution of replacing a trade in the market, if the counterparty defaults.

Pre-Settlement Risk Exposure Measurement

Delivery-v-Payment (DVP) Trading

Exposure on a DVP trade is calculated using the formula, Mark-to-Market (MTM) + Potential Future Exposure ("PFE"), PFE referring to the future replacement cost of a financial contract in the event that it has to be terminated by a counterparty default, or for any other reason.

Derivatives

The credit exposure for derivatives is calculated in the same way as above. Since the future value of a financial instrument is uncertain, and varies as a function of uncertain future interest rates, foreign exchange rates, equity prices and other risk drivers, the measures of PFE are defined in terms of a probability distribution of the value of the instrument at a future point in time. Two of the measures used are (i) Expected Future Exposure, being the mean of the probability distribution of future value. (ii) Maximum Future Exposure, being the value corresponding to a specified confidence level (e.g. 99%) at a given future time, representing an extreme measure of future risk that would be more conservative than the expected future exposure. Related to maximum PFE are: (iii) Peak Future exposure, being the maximum value of the maximum future exposure measure across all future points in time, indicating the largest value of the extreme measure of value over the future time-period. (iv) Average Maximum Future Exposure, being the average value of the maximum future exposure measure across all future points in time, effectively smoothing the extreme measure over the future time period. These measures are designed to reflect future exposure over the entire time-period prior to the final exercise date of a financial instrument, rather than just a single future point in time. The method used to determine exposure amounts is by performing a Monte Carlo simulation of the underlying interest rates, foreign exchange rates, equity prices, commodity prices and other risk drivers over the time interval up to each future point in time, and then using the resulting yield curve, and risk driver scenarios, to calculate the values of the financial instrument or portfolio at the future time.

Stock Borrowing & Lending and Repos / Reverse Repos

For these, exposure is calculated as the nominal value of the transaction less collateral value as determined by Mark-to-Market (MtM) + Potential Future Exposure (PFE). Limits on the nominal value of the transactions are also often set.

Settlement Risk

Settlement risk arises when there is an exchange of value (funds or instruments) for the same value date or different value dates, and receipt is not verified or expected until after the financial institution has given irrevocable instructions to pay, and paid or delivered its side of the trade. The risk is that the bank delivers / pays but does not receive payment / delivery from its counterparty. In this situation, the full value to be delivered is at risk. Different banks have different methods of measuring Settlement risk, this usually being either daily or on a two-day basis.

Examples of transactions where settlement risk is incurred are forward exchange contracts (except non-deliverable forwards); currency swaps; non-DVP equities and debt trading; and stock borrowing & lending, and repos / reverse repos where there is a timing difference between release of monies / collateral and receipt of collateral / monies. Pre-settlement limits are not accompanied by Settlement limits where there is no settlement risk, such as for interest rate derivatives, non-deliverable forwards, DVP trading, and where monies / collateral are received before release of counter-monies / collateral.

Bond and equity securities trading, and brokerage transactions, are processed via three main methods: (i) Euroclear (ii) Cedel (iii) Quasi-DVP. Euroclear is one of two International Central Securities Depositories ("ICSDs"); the other being Cedel. It is the world's premier settlement system for domestic and international securities transactions, covering bonds, equities and investment funds, its services being provided to major financial institutions in over 80 countries. In addition to its role as the leading ICSD, the Euroclear group also acts as the Central Securities Depository ("CSD") for Belgian, Dutch, French, Irish and UK securities. EMXCo is also part of the Euroclear group, the EMX Message System being the standard for fund order routing in the UK. The Euroclear group provides both ICSD and CSD services through its various entities. Euroclear Bank offers a single access point to securities services in over 25 equity markets and over 30 bond markets worldwide. Euroclear Bank clients benefit from an extensive range of settlement and related services. Euroclear also provides CSD services for four European markets, through the other entities of the group.

Cedel, founded in 1970 by participants in the Eurobond market, provides clearing, settlement and custody for a wide range of internationally traded Eurobonds, domestic bonds and equities.

Where quasi-DVP is used, this is achieved by contracting with a reputable bank with good custodian operations, which agrees to ensure that no monies or securities are released prior to receipt of counter-monies / securities, thus achieving an effective DVP settlement process.

TRADE CREDIT GIVEN

As with any firm, sale of goods or services with deferred payment by the buyer constitutes a trade credit risk.

POLICYHOLDER RISK

This is the risk that insurance companies and export credit agencies, from which policies and guarantees have been obtained, fail to honour these, leading to loss. Whilst it is conceivable that an insurance company might fail, it is unlikely that a State-owned export credit agency would do so, sovereign ratings quantifying the risks in this respect through probability of default range.

Where insurance coverage is obtained to limit certain risks (e.g. political and / or credit), these are generally obtained from highly-rated insurers with availability under approved policy risk limits (Contingent Risk). My book, "Insurance Company Financial & Risk Analysis" provides in-depth discussion on how to assess the well-being of insurance companies.

"KNOW YOUR CUSTOMER ("KYC") & ACCOUNT OPENING REQUIREMENTS

Prior to any credit limits or transactions being agreed or permitted, a firm will independently vet all potential new customers / clients, including legally-required money laundering checks, liaising with Compliance unit as appropriate.

NEW PRODUCTS

When new financial institution products are developed, they need to be approved by senior management, and integrated into, and supported by, the bank's risk management, operational and control frameworks. A new product will not be introduced unless appropriate line management and risk management authority has been granted to avoid unforeseen losses or operational problems.

CREDIT RISK APPROVAL STRUCTURE

Financial institutions approve credit risk limits in accordance with authorities delegated by the Board of Directors. Different organisations have different policies on this, but it is common for smaller amounts to be agreed under a dual control policy (a.k.a. "four eyes principle"), and higher amounts by a Credit Committee.

Depending on the size of the organisation, there may be a Standard Credit Committee up to a certain level of credit exposure, and a Senior Credit Committee for larger amounts, "amount" being usually defined as the total of exposure which the organisation has to the customer group: i.e. the Group Credit Exposure Level.

RESTRICTED & PROHIBITED ACTIVITIES

Financial institutions have rules on industries with which they will not transact, mainly on the grounds of the adverse publicity and damage to reputation this may cause, examples being financing of arms / weaponry and pornography. If the Relationship Management team wishes to do business with such firms, proposed transactions will normally go through a Transactions Committee and require Senior Credit Committee approval, or even Board approval. Needless to say, any activities which are illegal would be completely prohibited.

CREDIT RISK PORTFOLIO MANAGEMENT

The financial institution's Head of Risk Management will have delegated responsibility for ensuring that it does not incur excessive correlation risk in relation to customer groups, industry sectors or geographical sectors. This is achieved by setting limits for individual customer groups; country limits, and monitoring exposure to industry sectors, there being various techniques available, such as total return swaps and securitizations, to alter the bank's overall risk profile.

CUSTOMER CONCENTRATION RISK

Ultimately, the maximum credit exposure permitted for a customer depends on the creditworthiness of the client and the size of the financial institution's capital base.

CONTROLLING MAXIMUM EXPOSURE

This is achieved through use of "Credit Risk Thresholds", which are not credit limits as such, but maximum risk amount and tenor permitted to any organisation of a given rating. They are calculated so as to ensure that no credit risk exposure to a single customer group can exceed regulatory requirements on large exposures, in turn linked to size of your institution's capital base.

CREDIT LIMITS, OUTSTANDINGS & EXPOSURES

A "credit limit" is established during the approval process, restricting the amount of risk that the financial institution has to a given customer or group for the specific facility. "Outstandings" are the amount of risk existing at a given point in time, being the total amount of loan drawings, or calculated maximum PFE calculated for outstanding trades under a derivatives limit, for example.

"Exposure" equals outstandings plus the unused portion of committed limits. For uncommitted facilities, Exposure always equals outstandings.

Term / Tenor: For Banking Book business, the term of the facility is set by its expiry date. For counterparty risk exposure types, "time bands" or "tenor buckets" tend to be used to set tenor of limits and monitor utilisations, though this is not universal practice, particularly in smaller banks.

Subject to adequate documentation, netting of transactions and eligible collateral (i.e. of a liquid nature) is practised. If documentation is not satisfactory (i.e. because it has not been signed by the customer), transactions are shown gross, which leads to limits being used up more quickly. Different types of trading product are covered by different documentation as follows: (i) FX and derivatives - Netting: ISDA Master. Collateral: ISDA Credit Support Annex or Deed. (ii) FX - Netting: IFEMA, ICOM, FEOMA and similar local documents. Collateral: Margin supplement. (iii) Repos - Netting: MRA, GMRA. Collateral: Inherent within the document: repos are self-securing. (iv) Securities Lending - Netting: MSLA, GMSLA, OSLA, GESLA, ISLA, EMA and local variations. Collateral: Inherent within the document: securities lending transactions are self-securing. (v) For securities trading, a simple 'Terms of Business' letter is usually issued, with collateral not normally taken, except where the client is very weak.

CREDIT RISK RATINGS

All client groups on which the financial institution has credit risk should be rated, usually by reference to an internal rating model, or using external ratings. Individual legal entities within the customer group, on which there is exposure, should also be rated, either using the group rating (if parental support is assured) or by analysis of that entity's financial and business risk condition (if there is no assured parental support). If a facility is guaranteed, the rating of the guarantor is used. Tangible security or collateral cover is not factored-in to the rating even if it is so good as to completely mitigate a potential loss. The aim of rating the counterparty is to derive an accurate estimate of the probability of default of the customer, this being determined from analysis of the customer's financial condition, and qualitative factors, such as perceived quality of management; sector "riskiness" in terms of macro-environmental factors; the client's position within the sector, and competitive advantage. Bond spread, 5Y CDS spread, and share price data may also be used. Internal ratings may also be benchmarked to external ratings, though many larger financial institutions require that internal ratings be independently derived even if there are external ratings available.

An example of a ratings structure is:

Investment Grade: 1 (Excellent) = AAA (Aaa). 2 (Strong) = AA+/- (Aa1/2/3). 3 (Good) = A+/- (A1/2/3). 4 (Satisfactory) = BBB+/- (Baa1/2/3).

Sub-Investment Grade: 5 (Acceptable-Higher Risk) = BB+/- (Ba1/2/3). 6 (Marginal) = B+/- (B1/2/3). 7 (Unsatisfactory). 8 (Substandard - Potential loss, with provision being considered). 9 (Doubtful. Provision After Collateral Value). 10 (Loss. Full Provision Needed).

CREDIT RISK MITIGATION

TRANSACTION STRUCTURE

Financial institutions aim to structure transactions in such a way as to avoid unnecessary transactional risk. Also, legal netting is obtained where possible.

AVOIDING SUBORDINATION

Generally speaking, banks have a policy whereby provision of credit facilities to their customers does not put them in a materially worse position than the majority of other banks with credit exposure to the client. For example, structural subordination is generally avoided by not transacting with less desirable legal entities within a client group, such as non-operating companies (when other bankers are transacting with main operating companies), creating a weaker position in the event of insolvency. If exposure is to an effective holding company, for example acting as the Group's central treasury, this is acceptable on the basis that other banks / financiers are in a similar position. Also, banks will tend not to participate in longer-term credit exposures of a junior / subordinated nature, where other banks are in a senior position, creating a legally-subordinated situation.

TAKING COLLATERAL / SECURITY

In a similar vein, banks aim to avoid "clean" (i.e. unsecured) exposure to a client if other financiers are secured, except where facilities provided by other bankers are of an inherently self-securing nature, such as reverse repos; certain trade finance activities and leasing.

Security / collateral is also often sought from customers not externally rated or with sub-investment grade ratings, with sufficient haircut or loan-to-value ("LTV") for the assets provided, and insurance cover obtained to cover any potential weaknesses in holding security (e.g. fire, theft, etc.) Parental guarantees, or at least positive intention to support (for major groups), are usually sought for exposure to weaker subsidiaries within a client group. For smaller, non-investment grade groups, a legally-enforceable parental guarantee is generally obtained, the wording of this document being checked by legal counsel. For very large multinational organisations, generally with external ratings above A or equivalent, a reasonably-worded letter of comfort or letter of awareness, stating that the parent group has a policy of supporting its subsidiaries, will generally be acceptable. Much depends on the organisation's historic record in supporting its subsidiaries; whether the subsidiary in question shares the name of the parent group, and whether the subsidiary is core or non-core. Some large, creditworthy organisations have a policy of not issuing formal documents to evidence support for their subsidiaries, in which case verification is required that the group has not issued letters of comfort / awareness, etc. to other banks, and a view taken as to the likelihood of the parent allowing its subsidiary to default based on the "core", "strategic" or "non-core" importance of that entity. Verbal assurances should also be sought from a senior executive within the parent Group, these being documented in a follow-up letter with a request that this be noted at Board level.

Banking Book Business

Security / collateral for such business can vary widely, examples being: (i) A fixed and floating charge (or "debenture") over all of a legal entity's assets. (ii) A registered charge over real-estate property. (iii) A charge over debtors and / or inventory. (iv) Holding of documents of title to inventory. (v) A charge over specific assets, including securities and cash. The value of the security will be what it can be sold for in an insolvency scenario, so will tend to have a realisable or "forced-sale" value below book value. The bank will therefore assess this forced-sale value by applying weightings to the book value of assets for a fixed & floating charge security (e.g. inventory: 30% weighting; accounts receivable: 60% weighting; motor vehicles: 50% weighting, cash: 0%, assuming not charged to the bank, since cash will have probably gone in an insolvency situation, etc.), or for lending against specific assets, use a loan-to-value ("LTV") ratio to ensure reasonable coverage; i.e. With security in the form of a commercial property and an LTV of 60%, the bank will lend 60% of the current market value of the property.

Trading Book / Capital Markets Business

Such collateral tends to be of a highly liquid, high-quality nature, such as cash, government securities and quoted corporate securities, generally investment grade. Non-investment grade securities tend to be avoided, but may be acceptable in specific circumstances with appropriate haircut / margin; i.e. With a haircut / margin of 30%, the bank will lend 70% of market value, with either a top-up made via margin call if market value falls, or reduction in transaction exposure via close-out. In taking eligible collateral, it should not be materially correlated with that of the counterparty.

Portfolio Collateral Limits

A Portfolio Collateral Concentration Limit is usually put in place to control the amount of collateral that can be accepted from all counterparties for each specific issuer, and a Portfolio Issue Concentration Limit controls the amount of each separate capital markets issue, as a percentage of total issue that the bank may accept from all counterparties.

Counterparty Collateral Limits

A Counterparty Collateral Concentration Limit regulates the amount of collateral, for each issuer that a counterparty may lodge as collateral as part of a reverse repo / securities borrowing portfolio. An additional Maximum Cash Out Limit can be applied to counterparties that provide non-investment grade collateral, limiting the gross notional cash that may be transferred in a reverse repo / securities borrowing transaction to a counterparty against all non-investment rating collateral financed.

LEGAL CLAUSES & FINANCIAL COVENANTS

A good set of financial covenants (e.g. Net Debt / EBITDA; EBITDA / Net Interest Expense; size of Shareholders' Equity; size of NAV, etc.) are desirable within legal documentation, particularly for longer-term business and bilateral arrangements. Again, the ability to get good covenant protection depends on the willingness of other banks to accept weaker protection based on current perceptions regarding the firm, so a decision will need to be made on a case-by-case basis as to whether weak covenant protection is a "deal-breaker".

Similarly, in ISDA / capital markets documentation, suitable external ratings downgrade clause; cross-default / cross-acceleration clause, CSA threshold, etc. should be negotiated with the client prior to utilisation, as well as break clauses within trading confirmations. A break clause is where the provider of longer-term derivatives products is able to close-out the transaction after a given period of time if the customer's weak financial position warrants this. Break clauses are rarely exercised in practice, but can be a useful safety mechanism. An example is if a moderately sized, but expert, customer requests a 10-year derivative limit, but the bank considers 3 years to be more reasonable. In this scenario, the bank could agree 10-year trades, but have the right to terminate every three years (i.e. a 3-year rolling break clause). Agreeing break clauses can be difficult if derivatives are used to hedge a longer-term loan, the tenor of the derivatives needing to be in line with the term of such loan.

RECORDING RISK ON THIRD-PARTY GUARANTORS

Where limits for a client are guaranteed by a third party (such as a bank or export credit agency), the policy is that the risk on the guaranteeing third party should be recorded against the guarantor's name under the "Contingent" risk category, the use of the latter recognising the fact that recourse to the guarantor is largely a secondary risk. Exposure against the underlying customer is then usually shown as Nil, with an explanation regarding the guarantee.

EXPOSURE MONITORING

Exposure monitoring and control is crucial to a bank's successful credit risk management, as is the need to make information on limits and utilisation of these available to key staff and management to avoid unauthorised excesses, and to enable fast corrective action to be taken when these, or failed / delayed transactions occur. A bank's monitoring procedures tend to differentiate between two levels: (i) Intraday Monitoring: Whenever a deal creates a potential excess, the Front Office unit originating the excess has to apply for approval of the excess in accordance with temporary excess procedures before the transaction is confirmed to the counterparty. (ii) End of Day Monitoring: After deals have been confirmed and input in the general ledger system, an End of Day excess report is generated. If any excess appears on the excess report which has not previously been approved, senior management will consider taking action to regularise the excess and to avoid future repetitions.

LIMIT EXCESSES & FAILED TRANSACTIONS

To ensure proper front office discipline, it is normal practice that a bank will not ratify (i.e. provide post-transaction approval) for unauthorised transactions, disciplinary action being taken towards relevant staff if this occurs, a "three strikes and you're out" policy often being adopted.

Failed or delayed trades can arise for simple technical or administrative reasons (e.g. loss of certificates or other documents) rather than insolvency or financial difficulties experienced by clients. In such circumstances, the bank will (i) Determine from the customer the precise reason for the failed or delayed transaction. (ii) Determine whether the transaction can be executed in the future and when. (iii) Recover costs from the customer as covered by the documentation and market practice.

PROBLEM CREDITS & WORK-OUTS

All clients regarded as problematic, with a rating of Unsatisfactory, Substandard, Doubtful or Loss, are usually transferred to a dedicated work-out unit and / or handled by a work-out specialist. He / she reviews the files and documentation to determine the extent of the bank's potential loss, and why any risk mitigation techniques (e.g. security / collateral) are not effective in preventing this. He / she will also assess whether any mistakes have been made by bank officers in the process, reporting findings to the bank's senior management. The aim of the work-out officer is to protect the bank's position, taking immediate action to prevent any further potential losses, and developing a strategy to recover monies. The adopted strategy will depend on the specific circumstances of the case, issues to be considered being: (i) The integrity, skills, reliability and commitment of the customer's owners and management. (ii) Viability of the core business. (iii) Feasibility of the remedial business plan in improving business performance. (iv) The customer's business environment. (v) Inherent risks in continuing to support the customer's business performance. (vi) Availability of financial support from interested parties. (vii) Availability of additional security. (viii) Track record of the customer. (ix) Willingness of customer to work towards achieving agreed objectives. (x) Feasibility of proposed strategy. (xi) Anticipated "likely" and "at worst" outcomes if the bank realizes security / collateral. It may be appropriate for the bank to appoint an investigative accountant.

After assessing these various issues, the bank will classify the customer as either "retain" or "exit". A plan will then be developed, these being time and event bounded and ideally agreed with the customer. For "retain" customers, the action plan will focus on prevention of further deterioration, and restoration to a satisfactory risk rating. For "exit" customers, it will focus on prevention of further exposure, and repayment / clearance within optimum timing. If there is likelihood of principal loss, a recommendation is required as to provisioning in terms of impaired asset procedures.

COUNTRY RISK LIMITS

"Country Risk" (or "Cross-Border Risk") refers to the financial risks of a transaction relating to the political, economic or social instability of the country of a debtor / counterparty, and is over and above the credit risk of the latter.

Financial institutions have a country risk management framework consistent with potential and actual cross-border exposure. In line with the risk philosophy that substantiates the Economic Capital approach to risk-based capital management, the bank will aim for full integration of country risk within the main four risk categories of credit risk, market risk, operational risk and business risk. A bank's aim is to limit losses arising from adverse events in various regions and countries of the world, this generally relating to transfer risk, where payment or discharge of a transaction involves a flow of funds from one country to another, or through asset deterioration in a particular country. The bank therefore (i) defines country risk and where it may occur; (ii) sets control limits approved by senior management, and (iii) where possible, uses risk mitigation strategies for individual transactions and on a portfolio basis.

The main types of Country Risk are:

(i) Sovereign Risk: The risk of a potential restriction of assets imposed by a government. For example, a foreign central bank may change its foreign exchange regulations resulting in significant or complete devaluation of the value of foreign exchange contracts. It also refers to the risk of government default on a loan made to it, or guaranteed by it.

(ii) Transfer / Convertibility Risk: This is the risk associated with the possibility of a currency not being sent out of the country, usually owing to central bank restrictions or a national debt rescheduling.

(iii) Contagion Risk: This is the possibility that any adverse economic or political factor in one country has an impact on other countries in that region.

REMUNERATION

The primary reason for a bank being in business is to meet the needs of stakeholders, in particular to generate good profits for shareholders. This can only be achieved by ensuring that the bank's risk management practices limit losses, and by achieving an acceptable return on the risks being taken. In the latter respect, RAROC ("Risk-Adjusted Return on Capital") is a useful measure in pricing products, and determining whether a particular sector is one in which to operate. RAROC is generally calculated at facility and relationship levels, showing the profitability of a customer relationship at entity and group level.

RAROC is calculated as Net Risk-Adjusted Return / Economic Capital, where: (i) Risk-Adjusted Return = Revenue − Expense − Expected Credit Loss − Expected Transfer Loss + Capital Benefit. (ii) Net Risk-Adjusted Return = Risk-Adjusted Return − Tax (iii) Economic capital is the amount of capital needed to cover risks.

ROUND-UP

I hope that you have enjoyed this book, and learned something useful from it. All that remains is to put what you have learned into practice, the following two case studies showing how to do this, the first being for a major bank, and the second for a hedge fund.

Chapter 9
CASE STUDY 1: LARGE BANK LTD.

Customer Name & Nature of Business:

Large Bank Ltd., which is a global omni-service bank, with headquarters in Mauritania.

Stock Market Indicators

Large Bank has current market capitalization of MTD 27.86 billion. Its current share price of MTD 1.65 is in the bottom half of the 12-month range of MTD 121-264, possibly indicating the Market's discontent with performance, and also general weak economic conditions in Mauritania. With a beta of 1.56, the share price is significantly more volatile than the Mauritanian Stock Exchange.

External Ratings:

Large Bank's long-term bond ratings are BBB- / Baa3, with negative outlook, this being the very bottom of investment grade level, potential downgrade taking the bank into sub-investment grade territory. The recent change from "stable" to "negative" outlook is the result of difficult market conditions in Mauritania, which are likely to impact the bank's local business and represents a significant proportion of total operations.

Aside from this, there are negative pressures on the bank's intrinsic creditworthiness, including shorter-term profitability challenges, despite improvement in balance sheet metrics. Also, in the longer term, potentially higher and volatile wholesale funding costs could depress the bank's net interest margin (difference between interest income and interest expense).

Internal Rating:

Inputting financial and qualitative information into our internal ratings system produces a rating of 5, which is just below investment grade. It is decided that overriding this grade upwards to 4, to align with external rating, is, unwarranted in this case, particularly given the negative outlook.

Transaction / Limit Details:

Our medium-sized organisation is contemplating derivatives trading with Large Bank up to a USD 20 million PFE level (Pre-settlement Risk), with 5-year tenor, plus Settlement Risk for FX products of USD 100 million.

Our risk is that the bank becomes insolvent quickly, without time to instigate the collateral arrangements referred to below. The potential loss is therefore the mark-to-market ("MtM") value of trades, plus any adverse movements in prices during the close-out period, which is estimated at 14 days. In addition, we could lose up to USD 100 million for any settlement monies paid out for FX transactions (these not generally netted) before receipt of counter-monies.

Security / Collateral:

No collateral is envisaged for this exposure, unless external ratings fall below BBB-/Baa3, in which case there will be full collateralisation.

Of particular note here is that Large Bank is at BBB-/Baa3 level already, so a one-notch downgrade will mean that all of our exposure must be fully collateralized. However, Large Bank may not accept these terms, perhaps aiming to negotiate a trigger level of BB-/Ba3. Much will depend on how its ISDA agreements with other institutions have been worded, so we should be at least on equal terms with other institutions. If Large Bank is similarly required to collateralize a large part of its out-of-the-money MtM exposures, this will impact its liquidity position if ratings fall below trigger level.

Documentation Requirements / Terms:

The trades under the limit will be documented via an ISDA Master Agreement, with Credit Support Annex, key terms being a standard external ratings downgrade clause of BBB-/Baa3; cross-default threshold of 3% of total capital; CSA threshold of USD 20 million, unless at least one external rating falls below BBB-/Baa3 equivalent, in which case it will be nil, with a suitable independent amount taken. A "most-favoured nation" clause should be inserted to ensure that our organisation is pari passu (equal) with other organisations trading with Large Bank in terms of documentation terms.

Parental Support:

This is not needed since we will trade with the ultimate parent's treasury division.

LGD % (For each facility):

This is calculated at 30% for derivatives business, using our internal model based on historic losses for this product.

Internal Risk Controls:

These are in line with industry best practice.

External Regulation:

In Mauritania, the Bank of Mauritania has responsibility for monitoring the Mauritanian financial system as a whole, the day-to-day regulation and supervision of the Group being divided between the Financial Regulation Authority (FRA), which is established as part of the Bank of Mauritania, and the Financial Conduct Commission (FCC). Activities through subsidiaries in other countries are also regulated by local regulators. External regulation is considered very high quality and of world-standard.

Other Macro-Environmental Risks:

Large Bank is not exposed to unusual risks in this respect, with reasonable levels of insurance to cover most realistically potential events.

Micro-Environmental Risk (Competitive Environment):

Large Bank is a market leader in Mauritania, being one of the top three banks in terms of size. In terms of loan losses, it is relatively strong, but its profitability has been impacted more than average by regulatory fines for bad practices, including mis-selling of financial products. Its capital base is also relatively weak, but it is looking to address this problem with a rights issue. The bank remains highly regarded by the general public.

Potential Concentration & Event Risks:

Large Bank has no material concentration risks, other than on the Mauritanian economy, and is adequately covered by event-risk insurance.

Financial Analysis:

Balance Sheet:

Large Bank has a substantial balance sheet, with total assets of MTD (Mauritania dollars) 1,129 trillion as at FYE 31/12/X3, MTD 1.150 trillion when including important off-balance sheet contingents. This represents a reduction on previous years as the bank made efforts to dispose of non-core activities. As expected, the main component categories of the bank's assets were loans made (37%); liquid assets (13%) and deposits held with central and other banks (8%), derivative assets (29%) being largely offset by derivative liabilities through the bank's hedging process.

The bank's major liability categories were deposits received from customers and interbank borrowings (46%); other borrowings (18%), and the afore-mentioned derivatives liabilities.

In terms of maturity profile of loans given and core funding (mainly deposits received), the usual asset-liability mismatch is evident, but since retail deposits tend to be fairly stable, other things being equal, this is not viewed as a problem. Only if the bank's financial situation seriously deteriorates, and external ratings move into deep non-investment grade territory, could there be a run on the bank and liquidity crisis.

Income Statement:

Large Bank's main source of revenue is net interest received on lending, representing 54%, 45% after deduction of loan loss expenses and provision charges.

The latter appears to be quite large in percentage terms (9%), showing how relatively low loss levels (compared to total loans granted) can have a material impact on profits, the bank losing over MTD 2 billion in this respect in 20X3, though better than in previous years.

Fee and other income is equally as important to Large Bank in terms of revenue generation. Whilst returns on lending can be quite reasonable in the retail (i.e. personal) and small-to-medium-sized business segment, they can be very low for larger corporate and institutional customers, banks needing to bolster this interest income with fees and commissions through other services. Indeed, meaningful so-called "ancillary business" revenue can only be obtained by being on a large corporate's core banking list, with any financial institution not on this list having little chance of getting much business.

Personnel costs (46% of net revenue in 20X3) are a material issue for Large Bank, given its retail focus and large number of staff required to operate branches and internal processes. The bank is attempting to reduce this cost through branch closures and redundancies across its operations, as well as moving some operations to developing markets where staff costs are significantly less, but risks are higher. Time will tell as to whether this strategy is a good one in the longer term.

A fairly significant cost for the bank is non-loan provision charges, which rose fairly materially in 20X3 to MTD 4 billion (20X2: MTD 2.35 billion). This relates to regulatory fines and other litigation costs and payouts, which seem to be a regular feature of the bank's operations. If the bank could improve its activities to reduce these outgoings to a minimum, it would significantly improve its profitability ratios. Adding together loan losses and non-loan provisions, the bank lost MTD 6.123 billion in 20X3 (20X2: MTD 4.518 billion), compared to pre-tax profit of only MTD 2.073 billion (20X2: MTD 2.256 billion).

Profitability:

Profitability ratios have been low for some years, all showing that the bank is operating not far above break-even point. The situation would be much better if it could reduce its afore-mentioned loan and non-loan provision losses.

Personnel Efficiency:

Large Bank employs almost 124k people, mostly in Mauritania, this figure reducing as non-core businesses are sold and redundancies are made. Costs per employee have therefore reduced markedly, falling from MTD 106,386 in 20X1 to MTD 85,654 in 20X3, but net revenue generated per employee remaining fairly static. This improvement in average employee efficiency suggests that staff are being worked harder and / or salary payments and bonuses reduced, which could have either positive or negative implications in the longer term. The bank is reliant on its staff to be successful, so remuneration needs to be at least in line with the industry if good ones are to be retained. If it is not, and key employees leave, this will have a detrimental effect on the organisation, as will transfer of important operations overseas, where skill-levels may be lower.

Liquidity & Funding:

Large Bank seems to be becoming less efficient in terms of using its funding sources to make loans, Loans Made / Total Funding having a reducing trend, being 58.0% as at FYE 20X3 (20X2: 65.2%). This could be the result of the bank letting go of experienced lending staff to reduce personnel costs, together with sale of certain non-core businesses.

The bank does not have an over-reliance on inter-bank borrowings to fund its loan portfolio, though this is increasing, rising to 7.3% in 20X3 (20X2: 5.2%).

Of its total funding of MTD 737.13 billion, which reduced from MTD 937.41 billion in 20X1, mainly as a result of depositors' moderate concern at weakening external ratings, most (56.7% in 20X3) is in the form of demand deposits (which can be withdrawn by customers immediately without notice), with rising trend evident. This is a worrying sign, with the potential for significant cash withdrawals if ratings fall further.

Other borrowings, being bond issues; other external and secured debt via reverse repos and stock lending, is also reducing. With Large Bank's external ratings deteriorating to just at investment grade level, the bank's cost of borrowing has increased, and will continue to increase if ratings deteriorate further.

Adjusted liquid assets, being liquid assets and deposits made, less interbank borrowings, covered deposits received by 42.9% in 20X3 (20X2: 38.7%), the ratio being fairly stable, showing the extent to which depositors can be repaid from net liquid assets. This is largely in line with peers.

In terms of ability to repay all funding with liquid assets and deposits made, this has an improving trend, rising to 30.7% in 20X3 (20X2: 29.1%), again in line with peer group average.

Asset Quality:

Non-performing loans are low at 1.0% of total lending (20X2: 1.1%), indicating that Large Bank is pretty good in its lending and credit processes, 99% of its lending being successful. However, the bank needs to be very good given its relatively weak profitability, only a small absolute amount of loan write-offs significantly impacting bottom line.

Capital Adequacy:

Capital adequacy is pretty weak in the context of the banking sector as a whole, the Total Capital Ratio being just above minimum 8% requirement in 20X1 and 20X2, improving somewhat in 20X3 to 11.1%. This improvement arose through reduction in calculated RWA, this arising through sale of higher-risk, non-core businesses. Tier 1 capital adequacy is better, there having been a reasonable cushion above minimum 4.5% requirement under Basel III, being 9.1% as at FYE 20X3 (20X2: 7.2%). The bank acknowledges that equity capital base requires boosting, and plans a rights issue (sale of shares to existing shareholders) in the coming year.

Strengths & Weaknesses Summary:

Strengths:

- Strong market position in Mauritania.

- Adequate funding profile and good liquidity buffer.

- Capital adequacy has improved, and is now broadly in line with peers, though the bank wishes to bolster this with a rights issue.

- Good credit risk management, with low loan losses and provisions.

- Reasonable likelihood of State support if Large Bank were to become potentially insolvent, given importance to the Mauritanian economy.

Weaknesses:

- Large Bank's financial well-being is very much correlated to the well-being of the Mauritanian economy, notwithstanding its international operations.

-
- Some operational risk weaknesses, leading to selling of inappropriate financial products to customers.

- Earnings have been impacted by costs associated with running-down non-core businesses, as well as regulatory fines and litigation.

- High personnel costs, with efforts being made to reduce these through redundancies; branch closures, and moving of some operations overseas. This achieves short-term cost reduction, but may negatively impact performance, and increase risks, in the longer term.

Conclusion & Recommendation:

Large Bank remains investment grade, albeit just. If problems are experienced, there is a fairly strong likelihood of State bail-out, though this cannot be wholly relied upon, but makes sense given the importance of the bank to the Mauritanian economy.

The amount of exposure requested is small in the context of Large Bank's balance sheet, and the medium-term tenor is also acceptable in this context. The proposed collateral requirements, should external ratings fall further, are sensible, but are likely to be resisted by Large

Bank. We should at least be on equal ISDA terms with other organisations trading with the bank.

Approval is recommended.

FINANCIAL STATEMENTS

BANK ANALYZED:	LARGE BANK LTD.			
BALANCE SHEET	31/12/X1	31/12/X2	31/12/X3	
Currency:	MTD M	MTD M	MTD M	
Denomination:	1,000,000	1,000,000	1,000,000	
ASSETS				
Cash & Equivalents	10,436	11,876	12,435	1.1%
Government Securities	77,945	69,483	28,805	2.5%
Quoted Bonds	44,688	33,358	36,108	3.1%
Quoted Equities	38,968	38,300	76,830	6.7%
LIQUID ASSETS	172,037	153,017	154,178	13.4%
Deposits with Central Banks	35,187	29,795	41,011	3.6%
Deposits with Local banks	10,500	9,900	8,700	0.8%
Deposits with Other banks	39,422	42,111	41,349	3.6%
TOTAL DEPOSITS MADE	85,109	81,806	91,060	7.9%
Loans Made - Gross	621,016	559,520	427,404	37.2%
Less: Loan Loss Provisions	-6,955	-6,323	-4,488	-0.4%
LOANS MADE - NET	614,061	553,197	422,916	36.8%
TOTAL DEP + LOANS	699,170	635,003	513,976	44.7%
Derivative Financial Instruments	350,300	439,909	327,709	28.5%
Other Operating Assets	22,128	36,378	28,383	2.5%
TOT. OTHER OP. ASSETS	372,428	476,287	356,092	31.0%
Restricted Funds	1,282	1,210	1,011	0.1%
Available For Sale Investments	86,192	79,609	84,589	7.4%
TOTAL OTHER ASSETS	87,474	80,819	85,600	7.4%
Unconsolidated Subs. &	5,564	6,457	5,678	0.5%

Assoc. Property, Plant & Equipment	3,556	3,534	3,468	0.3%
Other Fixed Assets	1,267	1,302	1,356	0.1%
Goodwill & Other Intangible Assets	8,210	8,135	8,222	0.7%
TOTAL LT ASSETS	18,597	19,428	18,724	1.6%
TOTAL B/S ASSETS	1,349,706	1,364,554	1,128,570	98.1%
TOTAL CONTINGENT ASSETS (See Contingent Liabs)	20,894	22,169	21,712	1.9%
TOTAL ASSETS & CONTINGENTS	1,370,600	1,386,723	1,150,282	<u>100.0%</u>

	31/12/X1 MTD M	31/12/X2 MTD M	31/12/X3 MTD M	
CAPITAL & LIABILITIES				
Share Capital	19,887	20,809	21,586	1.9%
Other Non-Distributable Reserves	249	2,724	1,898	0.2%
Retained Earnings Reserve	33,186	31,712	31,021	2.7%
TIER 1 CAPITAL (CORE CAPITAL)	53,322	55,245	54,505	4.7%
Redeemable Preference Shares	2,063	4,322	5,305	0.5%
Other LT Capital Items	8,564	6,391	6,054	0.5%
TIER 2 CAPITAL	10,627	10,713	11,359	1.0%
TOTAL CAPITAL	63,949	65,958	65,864	5.7%
Demand Deposits Received	431,998	427,704	418,242	36.4%
Savings Deposits Received	53,464	45,124	33,967	3.0%
Time Deposits Received	55,615	58,390	47,080	4.1%
Inter-Bank Borrowings	29,132	28,978	31,038	2.7%
CORE FUNDING	570,209	560,196	530,327	46.1%
Debt Securities Issued	86,693	86,099	69,150	6.0%
Repos & Similar Borrowings	196,748	124,479	25,035	2.2%
Other Borrowings	83,755	87,068	112,617	9.8%
OTHER BORROWINGS	367,196	297,646	206,802	18.0%
TOTAL FUNDING	937,405	857,842	737,129	64.1%

	31/12/X1	31/12/X2	31/12/X3	
Derivatives	347,118	439,320	324,252	28.2%
Other Liabilities	1,234	1,434	1,325	0.1%
TOTAL OTHER LIABILITIES	**348,352**	**440,754**	**325,577**	**28.3%**
TOTAL CAPITAL & LIABILITIES	**1,349,706**	**1,364,554**	**1,128,570**	**98.1%**
Contingent Liabilities				
Acceptances & Performance Guarantees Issued	6,540	6,777	4,556	0.4%
Securing Guarantees Issued	13,567	14,547	16,065	1.4%
L/Cs & Other Trade Contingents	787	845	1,091	0.1%
TOTAL CONTINGENT LIABILITIES	**20,894**	**22,169**	**21,712**	**1.9%**
TOTAL CAPITAL, LIABILITIES & CONTINGENTS	**1,370,600**	**1,386,723**	**1,150,282**	**100.0%**

INCOME STATEMENT	31/12/X1 MTD M	31/12/X2 MTD M	31/12/X3 MTD M	
Net Interest Income	11,600	12,080	12,558	54.0%
Loan Loss Expense & Provisions	-3,071	-2,168	-2,114	-9.1%
NET LENDING REVENUE	**8,529**	**9,912**	**10,444**	**44.9%**
Fee & Other Income	16,076	12,747	12,829	55.1%
NET REVENUE	**24,605**	**22,659**	**23,273**	**100.0%**
Personnel Costs	-13,777	-11,933	-10,604	-45.6%
Non-Loan Provision Charges	-2,173	-2,350	-4,009	-17.2%
Other Operating Expenses	-5,787	-6,120	-6,587	-28.3%
OPERATING EXPENSES	**-21,737**	**-20,403**	**-21,200**	**-91.1%**
PROFIT (LOSS) BEFORE TAX	**2,868**	**2,256**	**2,073**	**8.9%**
Tax Expense	-1,571	-1,411	-1,450	-6.2%
PROFIT (LOSS) AFTER TAX	**1,297**	**845**	**623**	**2.7%**
Proposed Dividend	-532	-321	-243	-1.0%

RETAINED PROFIT FOR YEAR	765	524	380	1.6%

KEY RATIOS & OTHER CREDIT METRICS	31/12/X1	31/12/X2	31/12/X3
PROFITABILITY RATIOS	31/12/X1	31/12/X2	31/12/X3
Return on Assets	0.2%	0.2%	0.2%
Return on Risk Weighted Assets	0.4%	0.3%	0.3%
Return on Equity	4.5%	3.4%	3.1%
Effective Tax Rate	54.8%	62.5%	69.9%
PERSONNEL STATISTICS	31/12/X1	31/12/X2	31/12/X3
Average Number of Employees	129,500	123,500	123,800
Cost Per Employee	106,386	96,623	85,654
Net Revenue Per Employee	190,000	183,474	187,989
Employee Costs / Net Revenue	56.0%	52.7%	45.6%
Employee Costs / Operating Expenses	63.4%	58.5%	50.0%
LIQUIDITY & FUNDING RATIOS	31/12/X1	31/12/X2	31/12/X3
Loans Made / Total Funding	66.2%	65.2%	58.0%
Inter-Bank Borrowing / Loans Made	4.7%	5.2%	7.3%
Adj. Liquid Assets / Deposits Rec.	42.1%	38.7%	42.9%
Liquid Assets + Dep / Tot. Funding	27.4%	29.1%	30.7%
Demand Deposits / Total Funding	46.1%	49.9%	56.7%
Savings Deposits / Total Funding	5.7%	5.3%	4.6%
Time Deposits / Total Funding	5.9%	6.8%	6.4%
Inter-Bank Bor. / Total Funding	3.1%	3.4%	4.2%
Oth. Borrowings / Total Funding	39.2%	34.7%	28.1%

MATURITY PROFILE OF LOANS GIVEN	31/12/X1	31/12/X2	31/12/X3	
< 30 days	5,016	5,520	5,404	1.3%

30 days to 90 days	20,000	10,000	80,000	18.7%
90 days to 180 days	55,000	8,000	10,000	2.3%
180 days to 360 days	76,000	60,000	24,000	5.6%
> 360 days	465,000	476,000	308,000	72.1%
TOTAL LOANS GIVEN	**621,016**	**559,520**	**427,404**	**100.0%**
Re Balance Sheet	621,016	559,520	427,404	

MATURITY PROFILE OF CORE FUNDING

< 30 days	332,000	328,000	318,000	60.0%
30 days to 90 days	95,000	88,000	79,000	14.9%
90 days to 180 days	45,000	52,000	58,000	10.9%
180 days to 360 days	54,000	41,000	35,000	6.6%
> 360 days	44,209	51,196	40,327	7.6%
TOTAL CORE FUNDING	**570,209**	**560,196**	**530,327**	**100.0%**
Re Balance Sheet	570,209	560,196	530,327	

ASSET QUALITY RATIOS	31/12/X1	31/12/X2	31/12/X3	
Performing Loans	614,216	553,320	423,004	99.0%
Non-Performing Loans	6,800	6,200	4,400	1.0%
Split as:				
Sub-Standard loans	3,500	3,100	2,700	0.6%
Doubtful Loans	2,900	2,800	1,500	0.4%
Bad Debts	400	300	200	0.0%
TOTAL LOANS	**621,016**	**559,520**	**427,404**	**100.0%**
Non-Performing Loans / Total Loans - Gross	1.1%	1.1%	1.0%	
Loan Loss Provision / Total Loans - Gross	1.1%	1.1%	1.1%	
Loan Loss Provision / Non-Performing Loans	102.3%	102.0%	102.0%	

CAPITAL ADEQUACY RATIOS	31/12/X1	31/12/X2	31/12/X3
Tier 1 Capital	53,322	55,245	54,505
Tier 2 Capital	10,627	10,713	11,359
Total Capital	63,949	65,958	65,864
Risk-Weighted Assets	789,639	765,837	595,872
Risk-Weighted Assets / Total Assets & Contingents	57.6%	55.2%	51.8%
Total Capital / Risk Weighted Assets	8.1%	8.6%	11.1%
Tier 1 Capital / Risk Weighted Assets	6.8%	7.2%	9.1%
Tier 1 Capital / Total Capital	83.4%	83.8%	82.8%

| Total Capital / Net Loans Given | 10.4% | 11.9% | 15.6% |

Chapter 10
CASE STUDY 2: ABC HEDGE FUND

Customer Name & Nature of Business:

ABC Hedge Fund, incorporated in Delaware, is an alternative investment fund seeking capital appreciation through positive returns, being managed by ABC Investment Advisers LLC. Whilst capital appreciation is the primary aim, any potential losses experienced will be limited through diversification, hedging and various other strategies.

The fund may take long and short positions across various global geographical markets, sectors and companies, in order to benefit from those investments which the managers and sub-advisers think have the greatest chance of upward value movement (long positions) and those likely to decline (short positions). Primary investment categories will be government debt securities; corporate debt and equities (investment and sub-investment graded); real estate property funds; mortgage-backed securities; asset backed securities; loan securities, including collateralized loan obligations ("CLOs"), and currencies. The fund may also use derivatives of four main types, namely (i) futures contracts on securities, indices, currencies and commodities, amongst other assets; (ii) swaps, including credit default swaps, total return swaps and interest rate swaps; (iii) call and put options on securities and indices, and (iv) forward contracts on securities, indices, currencies, commodities and other assets. These derivatives may be used to enhance returns, or manage the risk profile of the fund. Fund managers and sub-advisers may choose to hedge, or not hedge, positions as desired.

Principal risks potentially impacting Net Asset Value ("NAV") essentially relate to volatility of the equity, fixed income, commodity, FX and other markets in which the fund invests; leverage strategies amplifying potential losses. These in turn are impacted by various macro-environmental risks, as well as risks specific to a particular asset type, including asset quality (e.g. invested companies' ability to compete), and extent of hedging strategies adopted (e.g. credit default swaps).

External Ratings:

There are no external credit ratings. However, the fund's "star rating" from Morningstar is a quantitative, backward-looking measure of past performance, being based on a fund's risk- and cost- adjusted performance over three-, five-, and ten-year periods, helping investors to assess a fund's track record relative to its peers. It has been assigned a two-star rating, meaning that it is in the weakest 22.5%.

Internal Rating:

The star rating is not a risk rating as such, being more of a performance measure. Our internal rating system derives an internal rating of 4 (Satisfactory) from the quantitative and qualitative measures used in this analysis. Although the fund's performance relative to peers has been somewhat weak, it is well-diversified, with losses being low in absolute terms.

Transaction / Limit Details:

ABC Investment Advisers LLC has requested that we, as a securities trading bank, provide DVP trading limits (debt and equities); derivatives limits (forex and interest rate); stock borrowing & lending and repos / reverse repos for the fund as Principal. ABC Investment Advisers, and the various sub-advisers, will be transacting with us as Agents on behalf of the fund.

Based on discussions with our marketing department, the following limits are proposed:

DVP Debt Trading: Pre-settlement: USD 8 million
                                Tenor: 5 days

DVP Equity Trading: Pre-settlement: USD 8 million
                                Tenor: 5 days

Derivatives: Pre-settlement: USD 10 million
                                Tenor: 3 years
                                Settlement: USD 20 million

SB&L: Pre-settlement: USD 2 million
                                Tenor: 1 year
                                Settlement: USD 15 million

Repos: Pre-Settlement: USD 2 million
                          Tenor: 1 year
                          Settlement: USD 15 million

TOTALS:

Pre-settlement: USD 30 million
Settlement: USD 50 million

No Settlement limit is required for DVP trading since, by definition, there is no risk in this respect, payments and deliveries being controlled.

The Derivatives Settlement limit covers FX only, there being net settlement for interest rate contracts.

The SB&L and repos limits are of a pre-settlement nature by convention, the reason being the inherently collateralized nature of such transactions, eligible collateral value being deducted from notional value in deriving net exposure. The settlement limits are there to cover timing differences between payment / delivery and counter receipt of funds and securities at origination and maturity. Utilization of the limit depends on whether the timing works in your favour or not, which is generally related to world time-zones and official confirmation of receipts and payments.

Security / Collateral:

No security or collateral will be taken except for that inherent within SB&L and repo transactions.

Documentation Requirements / Terms:

DVP securities trading will be documented via issue of a terms of business letter to the customer.

Derivatives will be under an ISDA Master Agreement, with no CSA, a fixed cross-default threshold of USD 10 million being set, meaning that any defaulting exposures with third-parties above this level will enable us to terminate / close-out our derivatives transactions. There are no external credit ratings, so no external ratings downgrade clause will be set, but the usual "material adverse change" clause will be inserted, theoretically (but rarely practically) enabling termination if the well-being of the fund significantly changes. We shall seek inclusion of an "MFN" (Most-Favoured Nation) clause, meaning that our documentation terms will always be at least equal to those in ISDAs with other institutions.

SB&L will be documented under a global securities lending agreement, and repos under a global securities repurchase agreement.

Parental Support

Neither ABC Investment Advisers, nor the sub-advisers, will provide any formal or moral support, our risk being purely on the underlying fund, ABC Hedge Fund.

LGD % (For each facility):

With no subordination risk, and using our firm's loss experience with similar entities, calculated LGD %s are as follows:

DVP Debt Trading:	5%
DVP Equities Trading:	5%
Derivatives:	30%
SB&L:	25%
Repos:	25%

Management Risk:

ABC Investment Advisers LLC has USD 5.4 billion under management, this reducing slightly from USD 5.6 billion three years' ago. The firm is well-regarded in the fund management industry, and remains so notwithstanding high-profile departures two years' ago.

As a result of loss of major talent to other asset management firms, ABC Investment Advisers LLC decided last year to outsource investments to 12 sub-advisers. Each of these has their own particular investment specialization, the largest current allocations being to DFG Capital, which specializes in credit longs and shorts (18.0%), FGH Capital Partners, which specializes in asset-backed securities (17.4%), and HJK Asset Management, which handles global equity longs and shorts. All of these companies are regarded as being experienced in what they do.

Internal Risk Controls:

We have visited ABC Investment Advisers' offices, and discussed management strategy and internal controls with senior management. The firm is able to produce information on the fund's performance immediately, including constituent elements. Information systems clearly promote diversification of investments, internal holding limits being set to limit concentrations and excessive correlations. No material weaknesses have been identified.

External Regulation:

Compared to some hedge fund jurisdictions offshore, Delaware law and regulation is strong, this attracting investors. However, fees charged to investors for this relative safety can be higher than elsewhere, the average management fee being 1.4%, plus an incentive fee of a substantial 20%.

ABC Investment Advisers, LLC, and the sub-advisers, are regulated by the United States' Securities and Exchange Commission ("SEC"). The Advisers Act is the primary law covering US-based hedge fund managers, this imposing substantive requirements on investment advisers. Other laws cover hedge fund managers' use of futures, options and swaps; the ability to purchase equities sold in initial public offerings ("IPOs"), and short-selling of equities during restricted periods.

Other Macro-Environmental Risks:

The fund and investment manager are impacted by wealth demographics and, from this and economic factors, the availability of cash available to expert high-net worth individuals for investment. The fund's ability to make a good return is also impacted by the economies of countries in which it invests, but the wide-ranging strategies available (e.g. short-selling) make market falls less of an issue. Indeed, the fund is able to perform relatively better in such environments for this reason.

Micro-Environmental Risk (Competitive Environment):

ABC Investment Advisers, LLC is a well-regarded asset management firm, as are the range of underlying sub-advisers. However, there is always the risk that key staff could move to other organisations, negatively impacting fund performance, as happened to ABC Hedge Fund, Inc, after the first year. The hedge fund industry is highly competitive, investors being willing to move their money to more profitable funds if poor performance is not rectified quickly. The danger is that ABC Hedge Fund continues to form below average, leading to investors selling their investments.

Potential Concentration & Event Risks:

There are no concentration risks of any note. However, based on studies of Delaware-incorporated hedge funds relative to those established elsewhere, it has been found that they are more likely to be liquidated owing to poor performance, which is a particularly-important issue for ABC Hedge Fund given its poor performance over the last two years, and its low Morningstar two-star rating.

Also, where performance has been poor relative to other funds, fund managers are somewhat prone to increasing risk in order to improve returns (risk-reward strategy). However, ABC Investment Advisers has informed us that this is not the strategy for ABC Hedge Fund, neither their managers, nor those of the sub-advisers taking unnecessary risks which might significantly deplete Net Asset Value ("NAV").

Adequate insurance has been taken out to cover "Acts of God" or terrorist actions which might impact the fund's and fund manager's / sub-advisers' operations.

Financial Analysis:

Performance

The fund was set up just under four years' ago, generating a return of +9.85% in its first year (20X1), reducing to +0.71% in 20X2, with a loss of -4.68% in 20X3, the best quarterly return during the three-year period being 3.17% in Q1, 20X1, the worst being -5.69% in Q3, 20X3. The latest loss in 20X3 was weaker than the benchmark XYZ Global Hedge Fund Index 0f -3.64%, and way below the S&P 500 Index of leading US stocks of +1.38%, showing that the fund performed worse than average. The reason for this was major talent being headhunted and moving elsewhere during 20X2, the replacement managers being unable to perform to expectations in that, and the following, year. Some recovery has been seen this year (2Q, 20X4), though still negative at -2.05 % in the half year, again worse than the XYZ Global Hedge Fund Index (-0.83%) and the S&P 500 Index (+3.84%). However, in the latest quarter, a positive return of +1.12% was generated, with gains from credit and long/short equity outweighing losses from merger arbitrage, event driven and global macro/ managed futures, outperforming the hedge fund benchmark (+0.35%), but remaining below the US equity one (+2.46%).

ABC Investment Adviser LLC states that, given the strategies adopted (mainly short-selling), the fund tends to outperform bond and equity indices during market downturns, downward value being significantly less than bond and equity index falls. Indeed, average bond price fall during periods while the fund has existed is -0.79%, compared to an increase in fund value of +0.19% during those periods. Similarly, for equities, during periods when equities prices fell, the S&P 500 Index dropped -1.77%, compared to the fund's fall of only -0.43%.

Balance Sheet

Portfolio assets currently total USD 724 million, and Net Asset Value is USD 659 million, gross exposure (long + short positions) being 139.9%, and net exposure (long - short positions) being 59.9%.

Current investment allocation is long/short equity (29.4%), long/short debt (18.0%), asset-backed securities (17.4%), merger arbitrage (12.0%), global macro and managed futures (8.5%), European event-driven investments - long & short (6.9%), other event-driven investments (3.9%) and cash / other miscellaneous small investments (3.9%). There is a wide spread of investments within these categories, the largest single long position representing 1.4% of total invested assets, and the largest single short position only 0.8%.

In terms of geographical spread, 45% is to the US market; 35% to European developed-markets, and the remaining 20% across a number of other countries and regions. Concentration risk on the US and Europe is not of concern, and other investments are well diversified geographically.

Leverage

The fund is permitted to borrow up to 10% of portfolio assets total, currently being USD 65m (9.0%). This is an acceptable level of risk.

Strengths & Weaknesses Summary:

Strengths:

- Well-regarded investment adviser and sub-advisers, and good internal controls.

- Well-diversified portfolio of assets, with no concentration risks or correlations of note.

- Good regulations, being Delaware-incorporated, and advisers being SEC-regulated.

- Limits requested are reasonable in the context of fund-size, NAV being USD 659 million.

- Low leverage permitted, being maximum 10% of portfolio, with current level at 9%.

Weaknesses:

- Relatively poor fund performance relative to benchmarks and peers.

- Possibility that the fund will be closed and liquidated if poor performance continues, but ABC Investment Advisers tells us that there is no intention to do this at the current time. However, if such a decision is made, closure will be in a structured manner, with all external contracts being carefully wound-down.

Conclusion & Recommendation:

Although the fund has performed weakly in the last couple of years, asset depletion has been low. Also, the fund is well-diversified, and internal controls are good. The fund is relatively low-risk, with low leverage permitted.

Limits are recommended for approval.

DISCLAIMER

The aim of this book is to provide a high standard of financial education to the reader, the calculations, ratios and models discussed aiming to give insight into the well-being of the particular firm being analyzed. However, when using this book, the reader acknowledges that the Author and Publisher cannot accept any responsibility for how the information is used to make financial and other decisions, this being the sole responsibility of the decision-maker. Also, while every effort has been made to keep the information accurate, the Author and Publisher cannot accept any liability for any unintentional errors. The reader should consider seeking independent advice before making (or refraining from making) any specific credit, investment, financial or other decision of material size. Companies and firms analyzed in the case studies within this book are fictional, though based on real firms with different names. Any similarity in names with real companies is purely co-incidental.

INDEX

A

acceptances, 48, 92
Acts of God, 26
add-ons, 39
Advanced Approach, 33, 36
Advisers Act, 145
agent, 28
Agent, 70
Agent - syndicated, 91
alternative investments, 11
amortizing loan, 17
ancillary business, 127
annual reviews, 52
Asian crisis, 80
asset conversion cycle, 51
asset funding, 10
asset management, 28
asset management firms, 70
asset quality, 28, 51
asset quality & composition, 72
Asset-Liability Committee, 94
asset-liability maturity mismatch, 47, 57, 58
assets, 45
assets under management, 71
Audit & Internal Control, 78
Audit & Internal Control Committee, 88
audited financial statements, 29

B

back office, 70
back-testing, 81, 83
bad & doubtful debts, 61
bad security, 67

balance sheet, 28
Banking Book, 18, 77, 79, 108
banking crisis, 20, 94
banks, 10
Basel, 22, 32, 47, 63, 74, 94
Basel II, 75
basis risk, 82, 83
Basis Risk, 79
Bermuda, 71
beta, 22, 121
Bilateral Loans, 91
Board of Directors, 23, 88
bonds, 11, 72, 78
break clauses, 114
British Virgin Islands, 71
broker-dealers, 10, 68
brokers, 68
bullet repayment, 17, 91

C

capital adequacy, 20, 22, 28
capital base, 72
capital conservation buffer, 40
Capital Ratio, 33
case studies, 12
cash flow, 51
CDO, 20
CDOs, 10, 94
Cedel, 103
central bank, 48
Chairman, 23
Chief Executive Officer, 23
Chinese Walls, 30
clean exposure, 111
CLOs, 139
close-out period, 19, 122
Club Deals, 91
collateral, 18, 27, 67

153

collateralized debt obligation, 20
collateralized debt obligations, 94
collateralized loan obligations, 139
commerciality, 61
commodities, 11
commodity risk, 79, 83
competitive environment, 27
Compliance, 70
Compliance department, 25
concentration risk, 13, 72
concentration risks, 67
confidence levels, 81
consolidated financial statements, 28
Contagion Risk, 119
contingent liabilities, 48
Contingent risk, 89
convenience yield, 83
Corporate Governance, 23
Corporates, 10
correlation risk, 106
cost-benefit, 74
counterparty collateral concentration limit, 114
counterparty risk, 88
country, 25
country risk, 118
Credit Committee, 88, 105
credit conversion factors, 38
Credit Default Swap spread, 23
credit limit, 107
credit risk, 88
Credit Risk, 33
Credit risk management, 88
credit risk mitigation, 35
Credit Risk Thresholds, 107
Credit Support Annex, 18, 108
Credit VaR, 82
cross-acceleration, 21, 114
cross-border risk, 118
cross-default, 21, 114
CSA threshold, 114
CSA threshold amount, 18, 21

customer concentration, 107
customer deposits, 47

D

debenture, 112
Delaware, 71, 146
delivery-v-payment, 96
Delivery-v-Payment (DVP) Trading, 100
demographic, 25
derivative trade profile, 17
derivative utilization, 18
derivatives, 17, 18, 20
Derivatives, 100
differences of opinion, 16
difficult conditions, 13
discounting, 92
discretionary counter-cyclical buffer, 41
diversification, 13, 86
diversify asset portfolio, 10
documentation, 20, 108
DVP, 142
DVP securities trading, 28

E

economic, 25
effective tax rate, 53
efficiency of staff, 28
eligible collateral, 18, 108
EMA, 108
emerging market banks, 62
emerging markets, 44
enforcing security, 19, 27
equities, 72
equity risk, 78, 83
equity stocks, 11
Euroclear, 103
event risk, 13
excesses, 85
exchange rates, 79
exchange-traded funds, 70

Executive Committee, 88
Expected Future Exposure, 101
expected loss, 43
export credit agencies, 104
Exposure, 108
Exposure At Default, 34
exposure monitoring, 115
external ratings, 11, 34
external ratings agencies, 44
external ratings agency, 16
external ratings downgrade, 21, 114
external regulation, 25
extortionate interest rates, 67

F

facility letter, 20
failed & delayed trades, 116
fair value, 51
Federal Reserve, 42
fee / commission income, 69
fee and commission income, 50
fees, 11
FEOMA, 108
finance leases, 19
Financial Conduct Authority, 68
financial controllers, 70
financial covenants, 21, 114
Financial Markets division, 97
financial measures, 65
Financial Services Agency, 68
fixed and floating charge, 112
forced-sale value, 112
forecasts / projections, 28
format, 14
forward gap risk, 83
Foundation Approach, 36
four eyes principle, 105
fraud, 75
funding, 28
funds, 10, 28, 70
funds under management, 71
FX risk, 79, 82

G

GESLA, 108
GMRA, 108
GMSLA, 108
Group Credit Exposure Level, 106
guarantee from third party, 115
guarantees, 109

H

haircut, 19
haircut / margin, 111, 113
hedge funds, 11, 70, 71
hedging risk, 77

I

ICOM, 108
IFEMA, 108
incentive fee, 145
independent amount, 21
independent assessment, 16
Information Barriers, 30
initial margin, 21
insider dealing, 30
insolvency, 57, 112
insurance, 28
insurance companies, 69, 76, 104
Insurance Companies, 10
insurance cover, 26
inter-bank borrowings, 47
interest rate risk, 78, 82, 83
internal audit, 70
Internal Audit, 25
internal controls, 10, 24, 68, 71
internal rating, 16, 17
Internal Rating Based approach, 34
International Central Securities Depositories, 103
investment strategy, 72
investment trusts, 11, 70
ISDA, 18, 108

ISDA / CSA, 20
ISLA, 108
Issuer concentration, 87
Issuer Risk, 95

K

KYC, 105
KYC checks, 99

L

L/C confirmations, 92
large exposures, 107
leases, 19
legal, 25
legal counsel, 20
Lending, 89
lending accuracy, 60
letter of awareness, 111
letter of comfort, 111
Letter of Comfort, 21
letters of credit, 92
leverage, 11, 28, 71, 72, 140
leverage ratio - Basel III, 41
LGD%, 22
liabilities, 47
liquid assets, 48
liquidity, 28, 51, 72
Liquidity Coverage Ratio, 41
liquidity problem, 47
liquidity ratios - Basel III, 41
loan agreement, 20
loan loss expense, 54
loan loss provision, 61, 62
loan-to-value, 111, 112
long positions, 81, 139
Long-Form Confirmations, 98
Loss Given Default, 22, 33, 34
LTV, 111, 112

M

macro-environmental risk, 25

management fee, 145
management risk, 23
margin, 19
margin call, 19
Margin supplement, 108
market capitalisation, 22
Market Discipline, 33
Market Liquidity Risk, 80
market risk, 77
Market Risk, 33
market risk controls, 68
Market Risk Factor Sensitivities, 79
Market Risk Factors, 79, 81, 82
Market Risk limit, 79
Marking to market, 80
matched-principal trading, 69
matrix analysis, 72
Maturity, 34
maturity mismatch, 10
maximum cash out limit, 114
Maximum Future Exposure, 101
mean reversion shifts, 85
micro-environment, 27
Minimum Capital Requirement, 33
minimum transfer amount, 21
mis-selling, 10
Monte Carlo simulation, 78, 82, 101
moral purposes, 24
morality, 24
mortgage loans, 47
Mortgages, 90
MRA, 108
MSLA, 108
MtM, 80
mutual funds, 11, 70

N

natural environment, 25
nature of business, 16
NAV, 11, 72, 140

NBFIs, 67
Net Asset Value, 11, 72, 140
net interest margin, 122
Net Interest Margin, 53
Net Stable Funding Ratio, 41
Netherlands Antilles, 71
netting, 108, 110
Netting and Collateral Agreements, 98
new products, 105
non-bank lenders, 67

O

operating leases, 19
operational risk, 74
Operational Risk, 33
operational risk controls., 69
operational risk modelling, 75
option risks, 83
OSLA, 108
OTC, 38
Outstandings, 107
Overdrafts, 90
Over-The-Counter, 38

P

parental guarantee, 21
parental guarantees, 111
parental support, 21, 111
peer group analysis, 28, 65
pension funds, 11
performance guarantees, 92
performance incentives, 11
periodic reviews, 31
permitted borrowing - leverage, 71
Personal Loans, 90
personnel statistics, 55
PFE, 78, 101
political, 25
portfolio collateral concentration, 113

portfolio issue concentration limit, 113
position limits, 81
potential future exposure, 17, 39
Potential Future Exposure, 78, 100
precious metals, 11
Pre-Settlement, 96
Pre-Settlement Risk, 100
Price Risk, 79
price-sensitive information, 30
principal, 28
Principal, 70
private information, 30
probability of default, 109
Probability of Default, 33, 34
probability shifts, 85
problem credits, 117
Project Finance, 92
projections, 65
proprietary trading, 50, 86
purpose, 18

Q

Quasi-DVP, 103
quoted shares, 78

R

RAROC, 22, 39, 120
rating, 109
ratings, 65
ratings agencies, 94
ratings agency, 31
ratings structure, 109
ratios, 51
reading the press, 31
real estate property, 11
realisable value, 112
regulation, 10, 25, 67
regulations, 68
regulatory fines, 10
repayment holiday, 91

replacement cost, 78, 100
repos, 17, 19, 142
Repos / Reverse Repos, 102
repos documentation, 21
re-pricing risk, 82
reputation, 74
restricted and prohibited business, 106
Return On Assets, 52
Return on Equity, 52
Return on Risk-Weighted Assets, 52
revenue generation, 28
Revolving Credit Facilities, 90
rights issue, 131
risk amount, 17
risk controls, 12
Risk-Adjusted Return on Capital, 120
risk-based analysis, 13
risk-weighting, 33
rogue traders, 68, 74
rogue trading, 74
roll over loans, 91
rumours, 59
run on the bank, 47

S

SB&L, 142
scenario testing, 77, 80, 84
Securities and Exchange Commission, 68, 145
securities concentration, 86
securities firms, 68
securities trading, 17, 71
securitization, 10
Securitizations, 93
security, 18, 67
security / collateral, 94, 112
security realizable value, 68
self-securing, 19
Settlement limit, 96
Settlement risk, 102

Severity, 36
share price 12-month range, 22
share price data, 22
short positions, 81, 139
short selling, 11
short-selling, 11
short-term deposits, 17
short-term FX trading, 71
Sigma shifts, 85
socio-cultural, 25
Solvency II, 76
Sovereign, 44
Sovereign Risk, 119
special purpose vehicle, 93
Special Purpose Vehicle, 93
SPV, 93
standalone rating, 44
Standardised Approach, 33
stock borrowing & lending, 17, 19
Stock Borrowing & Lending, 102
stock lending documentation, 21
stop losses, 81
strategy, 10, 11
strengths & weaknesses, 29
stress testing, 77, 80, 85
structured approach, 13
Structured Finance, 93
subordination, 36
subordination - legal, 36, 111
subordination - structural, 37, 110
sub-prime, 20
Supervisory Review Process, 33
supplementary limits, 81
syndicated lending, 17
Syndicated Loans, 91

T

tabulated financial criteria, 65
TALCO, 78
technological, 25
tenor buckets, 108
tenor of risk, 17

Term / Tenor, 108
Terms of Business letter, 20, 108
terrorist action, 27
Three Pillars, 33
Tier 1, 48
Tier 1 Capital, 40
Tier 2, 48
Tier 2 capital, 40
Tier 3 capital, 40
time bands, 108
trade credit given, 104
Trade Finance, 92
trade finance products, 19
trade finance risk, 17
Trading Book, 18, 77, 79
Trading Floor, 97
trading securities, 68
Transactional Committee, 24
transactional risk, 17
Transactions Committee, 106
Transfer / Convertibility Risk, 119
Treasury Asset & Liability
   Committee, 78

U

uncollateralized, 60

uncollateralized risk, 19
underwriting risk, 95
undrawn committed borrowing
   lines, 51
unfunded exposure, 89
unit trusts, 11

V

Value at Risk, 77, 80, 81
VaR, 77, 80, 81
verbal assurances, 21
volatility, 22, 72
volatility shifts, 85

W

weather conditions, 26
work-out specialist, 117
World Trade Center disaster, 80
World Trade Centre disaster, 74

Y

yield curve, 85
yield curve risk, 82

www.ingramcontent.com/pod-product-compliance
Lightning Source LLC
Chambersburg PA
CBHW070244190526
45169CB00001B/300